CLEAN AIR REGULATION

Steven Scott Young

1350 East Touhy Avenue, Des Plaines, IL 60018
(708) 635-8800

ISBN 0-934165-49-9
PRINTED IN THE UNITED STATES

Author's Note

This publication is offered as an aid to maintaining professional competence, with the understanding that the author, editor, and publisher are not rendering legal accounting or any other professional advice.

Due to the rapidly changing nature of the law, the information in this publication may become outdated and therefore the reader using this publication should also research professional and current sources of authority. The bulk of this publication is based on what is known in the legal profession as *black letter law*, the latter being defined as the basic concept or underlying definition of a specific regulation or law.

The views expressed in this book are those of a variety of authors and do not necessarily reflect the position of Cahners Publishing Co.

I gratefully acknowledge the assistance of Mary Anagnost in the compilation of this work.

<u>**TABLE OF CONTENTS**</u>

THE CLEAN AIR ACT: ORIGINS AND PRINCIPLES

The principal statutory authorities for controlling air pollution are contained in the Clean Air Act. While other federal environmental laws can be used to address some aspects of air pollution (e.g., air emissions from hazardous waste disposal facilities are regulated under the Resource Conservation and Recovery Act (RCRA), air contaminants in the workplace are regulated under the Occupational Safety and Health (OSH) Act, and the Emergency Planning and Community Right-to-Know Act (EPCRA) requires reporting of toxic air emissions), the Clean Air Act establishes comprehensive sets of measures to control outdoor air pollution throughout the nation.[1]

With the industrial growth of the late 19th century, air pollution became a serious local problem in many areas. The *Georgia v. Tennessee Copper Co.* litigation illustrates how virtually uncontrolled emissions from industrial facilities caused such substantial environmental damage that equitable remedies were imposed in common law nuisance actions. Municipal smoke abatement ordinances were among the first environmental regulations adopted in the United States. Chicago, Cincinnati, New York, and Pittsburgh were among the first cities to adopt such regulations in the 1880s and 1890s. A few states also adopted regulations in the 19th century, but it was not until 1952 that the first state air pollution control agency was created, by Oregon. EPA, Environmental Progress and Challenges 13, (1988); S. Edelman, The Law of Air Pollution Control (1970). Because of the enormous smog problem created by California's

---

[1] Robert V. Percival, Alan S. Miller, Christopher H. Schroeder, James P. Leape, *Environmental Regulation* Law, Science, and Policy [Little, Brown and Company, 1992] p. 760.

love affair with the automobile, in 1959 California enacted legislation requiring the state Department of Public Health to establish air quality standards and to determine what controls on vehicle emissions would be necessary to comply with them.[2]

Federal air pollution regulation began with the Clean Air Act of 1963, 42 U.S.C. §§ 1857-1857*l* (1964). The Act empowered the Secretary of HEW to define air quality criteria based on scientific studies. The criteria were advisory, but the Secretary could convene a conference of state and local pollution officials in cases where interstate pollution endangered health or welfare. In theory, the conference procedure could provide the basis for a federal abatement action and a cease and desist order. However, by 1970 there had been less than a dozen conferences and only a single enforcement action. J. Esposito, Vanishing Air 118-151 (1970).[3]

Congress first provided for direct regulation of air pollution in the Motor Vehicle Air Pollution Control Act of 1965. HEW was directed to establish auto emissions standards "giving appropriate consideration to technological feasibility and economic costs." The Agency established standards for model year 1970 that required roughly a 50 percent reduction in hydrocarbons and carbon monoxide. These standards became the baseline for further

---

[2] Robert V. Percival, Alan S. Miller, Christopher H. Schroeder, James P. Leape, *Environmental Regulation* Law, Science, and Policy [Little, Brown and Company, 1992] p. 761.

[3] Ibid.

reductions mandated by Congress in 1970.[4]

The final federal clean air law prior to 1970 was the Air Quality Act of 1967. This Act created a comprehensive federal program for the first time. HEW was directed to define "air quality control regions" reflecting the meteorological and topographical factors that govern air quality. Federal funding was available for states willing to create regional commissions, necessary where air quality regions crossed state boundaries, but none were formed. States were required to adopt ambient air quality standards (typically expressed in terms of a maximum quantity of pollution per unit of time) consistent with the federal criteria of the 1963 Act. The next step was state adoption of implementation plans to meet the standards, subject to HEW approval. The only mechanism for federal enforcement was the conference procedure created in 1963.[5]

The federal government made its first foray into the field with the Air Pollution Control Act of 1955, ch. 360, 69 Stat. 322 (1955). The Act provided for research and technical assistance and authorized the Secretary of Health, Education, and Welfare (HEW) to work toward a better understanding of the causes and effects of air pollution. The Motor Vehicle Act of 1960, 74 Stat. 162 (1960), expanded federal research support to address pollution

---

[4] Robert V. Percival, Alan S. Miller, Christopher H. Schroeder, James P. Leape, *Environmental Regulation* Law, Science, and Policy [Little, Brown and Company, 1992] pp. 761-762.

[5] Robert V. Percival, Alan S. Miller, Christopher H. Schroeder, James P. Leape, *Environmental Regulation* Law, Science, and Policy [Little, Brown and Company, 1992] p. 762.

from motor vehicles. T. Jorling, The Federal Law of Air Pollution Control, Federal Environmental Law (E. Dolgin and T. Guilbert, eds. 1974).[6]

The federal Clean Air Act is the principal source of statutory authority for controlling air pollution. Originally enacted in 1963 and amended in 1967, the Act did not provide for comprehensive national regulation until the Clean Air Act Amendments of 1970 were adopted. The 1970 Amendments established the basic program for controlling air pollution that remains in effect today. The Clean Air Act was amended in comprehensive fashion in 1977, and, after a long legislative struggle, again in 1990.[7]

Historical Background

Clean air concerns have ancient origins, as worries about air pollution began in the Middle Ages. The issue was first raised by the burning of coal at fixed locations. Animals were the primary source of transportation, and there was little concern about any pollution that they might create.[8]

The Industrial Revolution caused a number of dramatic changes; one of the most dramatic was the increase in pollution. The popular vision of industrializing cities correctly includes smog

---

[6] Ibid.

[7] Ibid.

[8] Timothy A. Vanderver, Jr. et al., Clean Air Law and Regulation, The Bureau of National Affairs, Inc., Washington, D.C. (1992), p. 1.

lying over these cities and plumes of smoke emanating from factories. With the advent of railroads, pollution from transportation (mobile) sources began to become a concern.[9]

The 20th century saw exponential increases both in air pollution and in concerns about pollution. The development of chemical, petroleum, and other industries added significant quantities of other pollutants to those produced by burning coal. The development of the automobile led to pollution that was extraordinary in comparison to previous pollution from mobile sources.[10]

In the United States, pollution control began primarily as a local concern. Localities struggled with the problem of smoke pollution, and later with other types of air pollution, with little success. Industry's own efforts to reduce pollution were probably far more effective than local government efforts.[11]

To understand why the Clean Air Act has become such a complex beast, it is important to appreciate its historical background. A useful survey of how the federal role in air pollution control evolved is contained in J. Krier and E. Ursin, Pollution and Policy (1977). An early history of the Act that emphasizes the many institutional actors that influenced its implementation is R. Shep Melnick, Regulation and the Courts:

---

[9] Ibid.

[10] Ibid.

[11] Timothy A. Vanderver, Jr. et al., Clean Air Law and Regulation, The Bureau of National Affairs, Inc., Washington, D.C. (1992), p. 1.

The Case of the Clean Air Act (Brookings 1983). William Pederson's classic article, Why the Clean Air Act Works Badly, 199 U. Pa. L. Rev. 1059 (1981), spurred interest in the development of the kind of permit program now incorporated in the 1990 Amendments. Craig Oren has provided the most detailed guide to the impenetrable Prevention of Significant Deterioration (PSD) provisions of the Act. Oren, Prevention of Significant Deterioration: Control-Compelling Versus Site-Shifting, 74 Iowa, L. Rev. 1 (1988); Oren, Detail and Delegation: A Study in Statutory Specificity, 15 Colum. J. Envtl. L. 143 (1990).[12]

The Evolution of the Clean Air Act

In 1955, the first federal clean air legislation was enacted.[13] That statute proved ineffective, and Congress enacted the Clean Air Act of 1963.[14] A significant feature of this statute was the first federal regulation of mobile sources--motor vehicles--and the fuels used by motor vehicles. This mobile source legislation followed earlier, pioneering California legislation. It was not particularly effective, which led to further legislation.[15]

---

[12] Robert V. Percival, Alan S. Miller, Christopher H. Schroeder, James P. Leape, *Environmental Regulation* Law, Science, and Policy [Little, Brown and Company, 1992] p. 763.

[13] The Air Pollution Control, Research and Technical Assistance Act of 1955, Pub. L. No. 84-16, 69 Stat. 322.

[14] Pub. L. No. 88-206, 77 Stat. 392.

[15] Timothy A. Vanderver, Jr. et al., Clean Air Law and Regulation, The Bureau of National Affairs, Inc., Washington, D.C. (1992), pp. 1-2.

The most significant statutes for present purposes are the 1970, 1977, and the 1990 Amendments to the Clean Air Act.[16] With respect to stationary sources, the 1970 Amendments created the basic statutory framework, and the 1977 Amendments effected a "mid-course" correction. The 1990 Amendments dramatically expanded regulatory requirements for both stationary and mobile sources in order to deal with persistent air pollution problems.[17]

Clean air regulation falls into two parts: the regulation of stationary and mobile sources. The interrelationship between the two will be explored later but at this point it suffices to note that they differ almost completely. It should also be noted that the 1990 Amendments radically expanded those aspects of mobile source regulation pertaining to fuels in both depth and breadth.[18]

THE CLEAN AIR ACT OF 1970

The Clean Air Act of 1970 was the first of the comprehensive, medium-based, federal regulatory programs created in the 1970s to protect the environment. Because most of these laws emerged from the same congressional committees, the concepts and language adopted in the Clean Air Act provided important precedents for much of the environmental legislation that

---

[16] Pub. L. No. 91-604, 84 Stat. 1676 (1970); Pub. L. No. 95-95, 91 Stat. 689 (1977); Pub. L. No. 101-549, 104 Stat. 2399 (1990).

[17] Timothy A. Vanderver, Jr. et al., Clean Air Law and Regulation, The Bureau of National Affairs, Inc., Washington, D.C. (1992), p. 2.

[18] Ibid.

followed.[19]

Notwithstanding the clear influence of earlier statutes, the Clean Air Act of 1970 marked a major change in priorities, emphasis, and approach. The slow pace of federal enforcement had become an embarrassment publicized by Ralph Nader and echoed in political campaign speeches. The Act replaced the system of state air quality standards based on HEW health criteria with provisions mandating uniform, national standards based on the criteria documents. States were left with the responsibility to issue implementation plans, but the newly created EPA was required to promulgate a plan if the one proposed by a state was found to be inadequate. EPA was also directed to set nationally uniform emissions limits for major new stationary sources. Finally, the discretionary process for control of vehicle emissions was drastically limited; Congress required a 90 percent reduction in existing auto pollutant levels by the 1976 model year, subject only to the possibility of a one-year extension.[20]

Why did Congress depart so markedly from its prior approach? No doubt political considerations played a major role. The Democratically controlled Congress stood to benefit, and Senator Muskie, the Act's principal author, was considered the leading candidate to oppose President Nixon, a Republican, in the 1972 elections. The difficulties associated with implementing the law were Nixon's problem. On the other hand, there was less

---

[19] Robert V. Percival, Alan S. Miller, Christopher H. Schroeder, James P. Leape, *Environmental Regulation* Law, Science, and Policy [Little, Brown and Company, 1992] pp. 760-761.

[20] Ibid., pp. 763-764.

opposition to federal standards than one might have expected. While the automobile industry was not happy with stringent regulation, it preferred a preemptive federal law to the possibility of inconsistent state regulations.[21]

Interestingly, another contributing factor may have been the *absence* of strong environmental lobbying groups. That absence may have made Muskie and Nixon face a "politicians' dilemma" that created incentives for them "to pursue a less than ideal outcome in order to avoid an even less desirable result." Elliott, Ackerman, and Millian, Toward a Theory of Statutory Evolution: The Federalization of Environmental Law, 1 J. L. Econ. & Org. 313 (1985). In this instance, Nixon and Muskie were arguably "prisoners" to a bargaining situation in which neither could afford to take the risk of being viewed as weak on the environment with the approach of a presidential race. Without a strong environmental group to sanction a "reasonable" bill, Elliott et al. argued that the two candidates could only show strength by proposing tougher and tougher legislation.[22]

As originally enacted, the Clean Air Act of 1970 was a complicated piece of legislation. It has become more so as a result of subsequent Amendments, including the major Amendments of 1977 and of 1990. The general structure of the statute, however,

---

[21] Robert V. Percival, Alan S. Miller, Christopher H. Schroeder, James P. Leape, *Environmental Regulation* Law, Science, and Policy [Little, Brown and Company, 1992] p. 764.

[22] Robert V. Percival, Alan S. Miller, Christopher H. Schroeder, James P. Leape, *Environmental Regulation* Law, Science, and Policy [Little, Brown and Company, 1992] p. 764.

has remained relatively stable throughout.[23]

In 1970, the federal government assumed responsibility for setting four major types of standards. EPA was directed to:

(1) establish *nationally uniform ambient air quality standards* (NAAQS) for pollutants that EPA determined came from numerous or diverse sources and that "may reasonably be anticipated to endanger public health or welfare" (these are called the "criteria pollutants" because they satisfy the criteria identified in §§ 108 and 109 of the Act;

(2) establish *new source performance standards* (NSPS) for categories of pollution sources that contribute significantly to health- or welfare-endangering air pollution (§ 111);

(3) control mobile sources--automobiles, buses, and trucks (§§ 202-234)--by establishing *vehicle emissions standards* and by regulating *fuel content* (in some instances, Congress itself has enacted the exact numerical limitations for mobile source emissions and fuel content); and

(4) establish *national emission standards* for existing sources of hazardous air pollutants, pollutants thought to pose a particularly acute

---

[23] Ibid., p. 768.

danger to public health (§ 112).[24]

The major responsibility delegated to--or left with--the states is the responsibility to figure out precisely how to achieve the NAAQS. Section 110 of the Act requires states to prepare, and to update, a State Implementation Plan (SIP) that is adequate to assure that each air quality control region within the state will come into compliance with the NAAQS by a specified date. If a state fails to prepare a satisfactory plan, the EPA is instructed to prepare one for it, as a last resort.[25]

CLEAN AIR ACT AMENDMENTS OF 1977

In 1977, Congress amended the Act to address the many areas of the country that had failed to come into compliance with the National Ambient Air Quality Standards (NAAQS). In Part D of Title I of the Act, Congress imposed a host of new measures designed to ensure that nonattainment areas would soon come into compliance with the national standards.[26]

Congress also adopted the Prevention of Significant Deterioration (PSD) program in Part C of Title I of the Act. The PSD provisions impose a complicated set of additional

---

[24] Robert V. Percival, Alan S. Miller, Christopher H. Schroeder, James P. Leape, *Environmental Regulation* Law, Science, and Policy [Little, Brown and Company, 1992] p. 768.

[25] Robert V. Percival, Alan S. Miller, Christopher H. Schroeder, James P. Leape, *Environmental Regulation* Law, Science, and Policy [Little, Brown and Company, 1992] p. 768.

[26] Ibid., p. 764.

requirements applicable to limit air pollution in areas with air quality better than the NAAQS.[27]

The most significant addition of the 1977 Amendments was the statutory separation of the country into areas that were not yet achieving the NAAQS ("nonattainment areas") and those in which air quality was better than the ambient standards ("PSD" areas, for "prevention of significant deterioration").[28]

Regions may be nonattainment for one of the criteria pollutants but not others, and frequently are. The significance of being designated nonattainment under the 1977 Amendments is that the state is required to enact a SIP that imposes strict limitations on the construction of new or modified sources that would affect air quality in the region and also to retrofit Reasonably Available Control Technology (RACT) (as well as any other pollution controls needed to attain the NAAQs) on existing sources. New sources must meet the toughest of all standards, those requiring Lowest Achievable Emission Rate (LAER), must show that any other sources owned by the new source owner comply with the existing SIP, and must offset new pollution from the source by ensuring reductions of pollution from existing sources (§§ 171-178).[29]

PSD regions are classified into one of three subclasses,

---

[27] Ibid.

[28] Robert V. Percival, Alan S. Miller, Christopher H. Schroeder, James P. Leape, *Environmental Regulation* Law, Science, and Policy [Little, Brown and Company, 1992] p. 768.

[29] Ibid.

each of which places limits on the permissible increases in pollution, over a baseline that is to be determined when the first PSD permit is received by the state. Major new sources must employ Best Available Control Technology (BACT) and supply advance verification, typically through the use of computer modeling, that the added pollution will not exceed the allowable increase, or increment (§§ 161-169).[30]

In addition, the 1977 Amendments added certain visibility protections in national parks and other federal areas where visibility is found to have special value (§ 169A).[31]

CLEAN AIR ACT AMENDMENTS OF 1990

The Clean Air Act was enacted in response to public concern over the dangers of air pollution. Increased urbanization, industrial development and expanded use of motor vehicles have resulted in mounting dangers to the public health and welfare. Since the problem of air pollution transcends state boundaries and local jurisdictions, federal leadership and financial aid were considered essential in formulating a cooperative federal and state program to prevent and control air pollution. Thus, Congress created a regulatory statute with a multifold purpose including: the protection and enhancement of air quality; the acceleration of a national research and development program to prevent and control air pollution; and technical and financial assistance to state and local governments in formulating their own air pollution programs.

---

[30] Robert V. Percival, Alan S. Miller, Christopher H. Schroeder, James P. Leape, *Environmental Regulation* Law, Science, and Policy [Little, Brown and Company, 1992] p. 769.

[31] Ibid.

The Clean Air Act Amendments of 1990 establish new provisions aimed at controlling acid rain and ozone depletion. They also expand the Act's criminal enforcement provisions.[32]

The Clean Air Act regulates both stationary and mobile emission sources. The term "stationary source" is defined in the Act to mean any building, structure, facility or installation which emits or may emit any air pollutant. The term "mobile sources" refers to motor vehicles, motor vehicle engines and aircraft. Title I of the Act requires the EPA to promulgate national ambient air quality standards for each criteria pollutant; i.e., an air pollutant which EPA determines to be detrimental to public health and welfare. Responsibility has been delegated to each state to promulgate plans to implement these standards, known as state implementation plans (SIPs). The SIPs must be reviewed and approved by EPA. Title I also requires EPA to promulgate regulations to control the emission of hazardous air pollutants. The National Emission Standards for Hazardous Air Pollutants (NESHAP) program regulates asbestos demolition, among other things. The Clean Air Act Amendments of 1990 amended the NESHAP provision by establishing a statutory list of 189 hazardous air pollutants for which NESHAPs must be promulgated.[33]

Mobile emission sources (motor vehicles and aircraft) are regulated in Title II of the Statute. Among other things, EPA is required to promulgate regulations regarding motor vehicle

---

[32] Andrew Lauterback, Civil and Criminal Environmental Enforcement (92-09.03) (Printed by CopyTech Printing, Inc., Canton, MA), pp. 331-332.

[33] Ibid., p. 332.

emission and compliance testing and fuel standards. The penalties for the acts prohibited under Title II are civil only. Nonetheless, numerous criminal cases have been developed under Title 18 of the United States Code. The cases involve noncompliance with Title II regulatory requirements where false statements were made or fraudulent conduct has taken place in connection with these requirements.[34]

Other relevant parts in the Clean Air Act Amendments of 1990 include: Title IV: Acid Deposition Control; Title V: Permits; and Title VI: Stratospheric Ozone Depletion Provisions.[35]

Although they are the product of more than a decade of legislative debate, the massive Clean Air Act Amendments of 1990 generated remarkably little formal legislative history. Because the conference committee did not complete its work until just before adjournment, Congress simply ran out of time to prepare an elaborate conference report. While the Amendments occupy nearly 100 pages of tiny print in the October 26, 1990 Congressional Record (pp. H13101-13197), the Joint Explanatory Statement of the Committee of Conference occupies less than 7 pages (H13197-13203). A more detailed explanation of the legislation was inserted into the October 27, 1990 Congressional Record by Senator Baucus, the floor manager of the legislation

---

[34] Andrew Lauterback, Civil and Criminal Environmental Enforcement (92-09.03) (Printed by CopyTech Printing, Inc., Canton, MA), p. 333.

[35] Ibid.

(S16969-16983).[36]

A useful guide to the 1990 Amendments is J. Quarles and W. H. Lewis, Jr., The NEW Clean Air Act: A Guide to the Clean Air Program as Amended in 1990 (1990), available from the Washington, D.C. office of Morgan, Lewis & Bockius. The guide contains checklists for compliance planning and appendices listing likely nonattainment areas for various pollutants, relevant guidance documents, the 189 hazardous air pollutants, and the potential source categories to be regulated under amended § 112.[37]

EPA has prepared materials and has hosted video teleconferences to educate the public about the provisions of the new Clean Air Act Amendments. The resource materials for these teleconferences include a 24-page summary of the new Amendments. EPA, Legal Winds of Change: Business and the New Clean Air Act. (Videoconference Resource Materials, Nov. 28, 1990).[38]

EPA regulations implementing the Clean Air Act, which are likely to expand dramatically in coming years, are found at 40 C.F.R. parts 50-87.[39]

---

[36] Robert V. Percival, Alan S. Miller, Christopher H. Schroeder, James P. Leape, *Environmental Regulation* Law, Science, and Policy [Little, Brown and Company, 1992] p. 762.

[37] Ibid., pp. 762-763.

[38] Ibid., p. 763.

[39] Robert V. Percival, Alan S. Miller, Christopher H. Schroeder, James P. Leape, *Environmental Regulation* Law,

After enactment of the 1977 Amendments, 13 years passed before the Clean Air Act again was amended in comprehensive fashion. As the new deadlines set by the 1977 Amendments came and went, experience with the existing Act made the most convincing case for new legislation. However, the Reagan Administration's ideological opposition to regulation combined with severe regional splits within Congress over acid rain controls produced legislative gridlock. It took a new administration and key leadership changes in Congress to finally break the deadlock with the enactment of the Clean Air Act Amendments of 1990.[40]

A fascinating account of the political jockeying that ultimately produced the Clean Air Act Amendments of 1990 is provided in J. Edelson, A Win for Clean Air, Envtl. Forum 10-17 (Jan.-Feb. 1991). Key events in this saga included the following: In the summer of 1989, President Bush delivered on his campaign pledge to send comprehensive clean air legislation to Congress. The Bush Administration proposal included many far-reaching provisions, including a 10-million-ton-per-year reduction in sulfur dioxide emissions to combat acid rain, provisions to reduce emissions of hazardous air pollutants by 85 percent, and a clean fuels program that shocked many industry lobbyists. With the leadership in Congress committed to enacting a new law (Robert Byrd of West Virginia, who had opposed acid rain controls for fear of harming his state's coal industry, had been replaced as Senate Majority Leader by George Mitchell of Maine), the prospects for a new Clean Air Act had improved to the point that

Science, and Policy [Little, Brown and Company, 1992] p. 763.

[40] Ibid., p. 765.

industry no longer believed that it could block the legislation.[41]

The Senate Environment and Public Works Committee acted quickly in the fall of 1989. Dominated by environmentally minded senators, the committee reported out a bill with provisions for dealing with ozone nonattainment, acid rain, and hazardous air pollutants that were far more stringent than the administration's bill. Facing the threat of a filibuster by conservative Republicans, Senator Mitchell began six weeks of marathon closed-door negotiations with the administration and a group of senators called the Group of 15. Both industry and environmental lobbyists were excluded from the negotiations, which produced an agreement on a more moderate bill that the participants agreed not to amend on the Senate floor.[42]

During House committee markup in September 1989, a bitter battle broke out between Detroit-area Congressman John Dingell, the powerful chairman of the House Energy and Commerce Committee and an auto industry ally, and Los Angeles area Congressman Henry Waxman, chairman of that committee's Health and Environment subcommittee and a champion of strict air pollution controls. A compromise ultimately was reached that provided for stringent new auto emission standards but delayed their implementation. However, a dispute concerning how to ease the burden of new acid rain controls on Midwestern utilities

---

[41] Robert V. Percival, Alan S. Miller, Christopher H. Schroeder, James P. Leape, *Environmental Regulation* Law, Science, and Policy [Little, Brown and Company, 1992] p. 765.

[42] Robert V. Percival, Alan S. Miller, Christopher H. Schroeder, James P. Leape, *Environmental Regulation* Law, Science, and Policy [Little, Brown and Company, 1992] p. 765.

blocked the legislation's progress for several months.[43]

After narrowly defeating an amendment to relax provisions establishing a national permit program for sources of air pollution, the Senate overwhelmingly approved its bill on April 3, 1990. The House approved its version of the bill by an overwhelming margin on May 23, 1990. A conference committee of 7 senators and 140 House members then began months of negotiations to agree on a single bill. For the most part, the negotiations took place behind closed doors. As one of the negotiators noted, "The legislation was so intricate, so complicated, so divided on geographic, political, and economic levels, it would have been nearly impossible to publicly debate all the issues." By the time Congress recessed in August 1990, the conferees had only succeeded in reaching agreement on one relatively uncontroversial topic--phasing out ozone-depleting chlorofluorocarbons.[44]

Thus in the end the resolution of more than a decade of intense debate turned on political maneuvering in a conference committee sometimes holding all-night meetings throughout the last eight weeks of the session. Facing a drop-dead deadline, the conference committee met until 5:00 a.m. on October 22, 1990. The result was a massive body of complicated legislation for which there is virtually no formal legislative history because there was no time to prepare a conference report. The House approved the conference bill by a vote of 401-25 on October 26. The Senate concurred by a vote of 89-10 on October 27. President Bush

---

[43] Ibid., pp. 765-766.

[44] Robert V. Percival, Alan S. Miller, Christopher H. Schroeder, James P. Leape, Environmental Regulation Law, Science, and Policy [Little, Brown and Company, 1992] p. 766.

signed the legislation on November 15, 1990.[45]

The 1990 Amendments address several important deficiencies in the prior Act by imposing new requirements for areas out of compliance with air quality standards, a new program to control hazardous air pollutants, an acid rain control program, and new controls on mobile sources and the fuels they burn. The 700-page bill that resulted has been termed "one of the most complex pieces of regulatory legislation . . . ever adopted, and one of the most impenetrable." Nickel, Now, the Race to Regulate, 1991 Envtl. Forum 18-22 (Jan.-Feb. 1991). The Amendments imply another round of federal regulation, state implementation, and source compliance with potential for litigation in each state. The EPA is mandated to complete more than 100 rulemakings within two years, including the creation of a new permit program for existing stationary sources. One important amendment created a clean fuels program for mobile sources. For a useful overview, see J. Quarles and W. Lewis, The NEW Clean Air Act: A Guide to the Clean Air Program as Amended in 1990 (1990). The Amendments continue the "leapfrog" relationship of the federal environmental statutes, in which the experience gained from one statute is subsequently incorporated in others. Jorling, *The Federal Law of Air Pollution Control*, in Federal Environmental Law 1058, 1060 (E. Dolgin and T. Guilbert, eds. 1974).[46]

The 1990 Amendments also reflect several potentially

---

[45] Ibid.

[46] Robert V. Percival, Alan S. Miller, Christopher H. Schroeder, James P. Leape, *Environmental Regulation* Law, Science, and Policy [Little, Brown and Company, 1992] pp. 766-767.

significant conceptual adjustments. One involves an expanded deployment of incentive-based regulatory techniques, most notably the acid rain reduction program. A second involves the recognition that end-of-the-pipe controls, whether they be at the end of an automobile tailpipe or at the end of a factory's smokestack, are going to be inadequate to achieve the NAAQS in some major population centers. So, for example, Title I of the Amendments requires some nonattainment areas to implement work-related vehicle trip reduction programs (such as car and van pooling), to participate in a clean fuels program, or to require utilities to switch to low-pollution fuels. Likewise, Title II, in addition to making changes in existing emissions standards for new vehicles, also implements a clean fuels program to ensure the availability of alternative fuels for new production vehicles, as well as instituting a program to encourage the development of low-emissions vehicles.[47]

AIR EMISSIONS

A. Asbestos Removal Under the Clean Air Act

1. Asbestos fibers, when released into the atmosphere, can be breathed into the lungs and cause asbestosis and mesothelioma, a form of cancer.

2. Asbestos was widely used as insulating material in buildings. Exposure comes when a building is allowed to deteriorate, or when a building is

---

[47] Robert V. Percival, Alan S. Miller, Christopher H. Schroeder, James P. Leape, *Environmental Regulation* Law, Science, and Policy [Little, Brown and Company, 1992] p. 769.

renovated or demolished. EPA regulations require prior notice before demolition or renovation.

3. Liability for compliance is strict for both the owner of the property as well as the contractor.

4. There is a certain amount of public hysteria associated with asbestos, and sometimes activists seek removal of all asbestos, regardless of the actual conditions of exposure. Renovation to remove asbestos can be very expensive and, in some circumstances, can increase exposure.

5. Asbestos removal must be done with a high degree of care, and many contractors do not do a good job. Failure to assure proper handling can result in liability for toxic torts as well as statutory liability.

6. Asbestos is a hazardous substance, subject to Superfund liability for disposal at a site which is later abandoned. The ultimate disposal site of wastes from renovation or demolition is an important factor in potential liability.

B. <u>Radon</u>

1. Radon is a colorless, odorless gas that contains naturally occurring alpha particle (short wave length) radiation found in various soils that has been found to leak into and accumulate in harmful amounts inside homes and buildings.

2. EPA estimates that radon is responsible for 5,000 - 30,000 cases of lung cancer yearly.

3. EPA does not have a regulatory program; instead EPA has published a recommended "action level" of 4 picocuries per liter (pCi/1). EPA also has published information on the causes of high radon levels, and remediation actions home and building owners may take.

4. There is no way to predict which particular homes or buildings will contain high levels of radon; EPA has found high levels of radon to occur on a random but frequent basis throughout the country. The area around Washington, D.C., the Reading Prong Area of Pennsylvania, and Delaware are known areas where high radon levels have been found.

5. The law of liability for selling real estate containing high levels of radon is in its infancy. However, many prudent sellers and buyers are beginning to routinely test for radon prior to closing, to determine whether there are any hidden hazards. Testing is cheap and preventive action makes sense.

6. If high radon levels are found, remediation efforts can range from the very cheap and easy to the very expensive.

C. Sick Building Syndrome

1. There is a growing awareness that some internal

building environments contain sufficient chemicals and poor enough ventilation to create acute and chronic adverse health effects in the occupants, a condition known as the "sick building" syndrome.

2. The causes of "sick building" may be many: poor ventilation, high concentrations of chemicals from carpet, furniture, etc., such as formaldehyde; poorly functioning boilers or heaters, giving off high concentrations of carbon monoxide; indirect exposures from smokers, and so on. Legionnaire's disease is an example of another public health problem caused by the construction or operation of a building (in that case, linked to cooling water tower operation).

3. Where it occurs, the solution can range from the simple, cheap and easy to the complex, puzzling and difficult.

4. Some legislative proposals for regulatory approaches have been introduced in Congress, but EPA and other federal agencies do not yet have a regulatory program. Their approach, still in its infancy, is to provide research and information to the private sector.

5. The "sick building" syndrome may affect the habitability of the office space, and may create significant threats to the health of the occupants.

D. <u>Discharges to Outdoor Air</u>

1. The Clean Air Act establishes a comprehensive, complex and detailed regulatory regime for discharges of air pollutants, involving local, state and federal governments.

2. The federal government establishes National Ambient Air Quality Standards that are protective of health and welfare, and states must develop and enforce State Implementation Plans which establish the specific rules that apply to new and existing sources so that overall the air quality standards will be obtained.

3. If a state fails to develop or implement an appropriate State Implementation Plan, the affected area is subject to sanctions, including increased emission offset requirements for new or modified sources and cutoffs in federal funds for sewage treatment, highways, and state air pollution control agencies. In addition, EPA may have to step in and develop its own plan for attainment.

4. Over 70 areas of the country (virtually every major city) have failed to meet the required air quality standards. Recent amendments to the Clean Air Act single out these areas and those areas that fail to meet future air quality attainment goals for a cascading series of increasingly stringent regulations that will be applied progressively to virtually all sources of air emissions until the National Ambient Air Quality Standards are attained.

5. Controls are being applied to smaller and smaller sources, and many states and localities are being forced to come to grips with the effects of air pollution resulting from land use, transportation and development policies.

6. Sources subject to federal standards under the Clean Air Act will be required to obtain an operating permit, which codifies the various standards and restrictions applicable to the source under the Act.

7. In upcoming years, the automobile and oil industries will face increased motor vehicle fuel and emissions standards.

8. The list of regulated air toxics has been and will continue to be greatly expanded, subjecting numerous new source categories to technologically-based hazardous emissions standards.

9. The Clean Air Act Amendments will establish increasingly stringent limits on sulfur dioxide emissions in an attempt to control acid rain. However, individual sources such as coal-fueled power plants will be able to trade emission rights. Such transferable emission allowances represent an innovative attempt to introduce market-based incentives into pollution control.

10. Compliance costs can be quite high, and non-compliance can bring large civil, criminal, and administrative penalties.

EPA or state officers may soon be authorized to issue "field citations" for minor violations.

11. New development especially can be affected because of the requirement to obtain a permit prior to construction which demonstrates stringent technological controls, as well as compensating emissions offsets from other sources.

12. The recent amendments to the Clean Air Act will further restrict air emissions to levels that some industrial facilities may not be able to achieve and thereby require many businesses to curtail their operations or shut down entirely.

CRIMINAL PROVISIONS OF THE CLEAN AIR ACT

A. Violations Prior to the Clean Air Act Amendments of 1990

Section 113(c)(1) of the Clean Air Act, 42 U.S.C. § 7413(c)(1), reads as follows:

Any person who knowingly:

(A) violates any requirement of an applicable implementation plan (i) during any period of federally assumed enforcement, or (ii) more than 30 days after having been notified by the Administrator under subsection (a)(1) of this section that such person is violating such requirement; or

(B) violates or fails or refuses to comply with any order under § 7419 of this title or under subsection (a) or (d) of this section; or

(C) violates §§ 7411(e), 7412(c) of this title; or

(D) violates any requirement of § 119(g) (as in effect before August 7, 1977), subsection (b)(7) or (d)(5) of § 7420 of this title (relating to noncompliance penalties), or any requirement of part B of this subchapter (relating to ozone)

shall be punished by a fine of not more than $25,000 per day of violation, or by imprisonment for not more than 1 year, or both. If the conviction is for a violation committed after the first conviction of such person under this paragraph, punishment shall be a fine of not more than $50,000 per day of violation, or by imprisonment for not more than 2 years, or by both.[48]

Section 113(c)(2) reads as follows:

Any person who knowingly makes any false statement, representation, or certification in any application, record, report, plan, or other document filed or required to be

---

[48] Andrew Lauterback, Civil and Criminal Environmental Enforcement (92-09.03) (Printed by CopyTech Printing, Inc., Canton, MA), pp. 333-334.

maintained under this chapter or who falsifies, tampers with, or knowingly renders inaccurate any monitoring device or method required to be maintained under this chapter; shall upon conviction, be punished by a fine of not more than $10,000, or by imprisonment for not more than 6 months, or by both.[49]

B. Offenses Under the Clean Air Act Amendments of 1990

The 1990 Amendments add § 113(h) which changes the definition of "person" under the Act, and is unprecedented in federal environmental law. It limits the potential for prosecuting lower-level employees by allowing them, under certain circumstances, to claim they were acting under orders from senior management.[50]

Section 113(c)(1) now provides for felony-level punishment for knowing violations of Title I provisions. The elements are the same as in the prior Act.[51]

Section 113(c)(2) now provides imprisonment of up to 2 years for knowingly making false statements in any document required to be filed or maintained under the Act, or tampering

---

[49] Andrew Lauterback, Civil and Criminal Environmental Enforcement (92-09.03) (Printed by CopyTech Printing, Inc., Canton, MA), p. 334.

[50] Ibid., p. 335.

[51] Ibid.

with monitoring equipment.[52]

The Amendments also add two new criminal provisions: Section 113(c)(4): negligent endangerment; and Section 113(c)(5): knowing endangerment. The elements are similar to the knowing endangerment provisions in both RCRA and CWA, but the scienter requirements in § 113(c)(4) is negligence. Moreover, § 113(c)(4) provides for misdemeanor penalties, whereas § 113(c)(5) provides up to 15 years imprisonment. Fines under both provisions are determined under Title 18 U.S.C. § 3571, except the Act provides for a maximum penalty of $1 million for organizational defendants.[53]

The Political Nature of Clean Air Issues

Air pollution is, first and foremost, a political issue. When the question concerns the impact of pollution from "my" activities on "our" air, the relative rights of the various parties and of the general public come into stark conflict. This presents the type of situation that is political with a small "p": it is something people are concerned about and therefore something to which our political system is supposed to respond.[54]

---

[52] Ibid.

[53] Andrew Lauterback, Civil and Criminal Environmental Enforcement (92-09.03) (Printed by CopyTech Printing, Inc., Canton, MA), p. 335.

[54] Timothy A. Vanderver, Jr. et al., Clean Air Law and Regulation, The Bureau of National Affairs, Inc., Washington, D.C. (1992), p. 2.

Politics intrudes in the air pollution debate in a number of other ways, some of which are cross-cutting. First, in the traditional sense, it is a subject of conflict between Democrats and Republicans, with Democrats generally claiming the environmental high ground. It is also an issue over which politicians fight, regardless of party, as the legislative process leading to the 1990 Amendments made clear. A third type of political issue involves questions concerning relationships among federal, state, and local governments.[55]

Perhaps more interesting than these political face-offs is the politics of region against region and, to a lesser extent, of state against state. The classic example of such a conflict was the acid rain debate with the midwest and northeast regions noisily arguing their respective positions. Closely related was the debate between low-sulfur coal areas (i.e., the West) and high-sulfur coal areas (West Virginia) over the best way of reducing sulfur dioxide emissions from the burning of coal.[56]

As time passes, confrontations between different industries will become more intense and will be brought to Congress, the statehouses, and the federal and state regulatory agencies. Industries have already squared off, as illustrated by the automotive versus petroleum industry battle over onboard (vehicle-based) control systems or "stage 2" service station pump controls. These confrontations will become more frequent and more significant as increasing population increases pollution potential

---

[55] Timothy A. Vanderver, Jr. et al., Clean Air Law and Regulation, The Bureau of National Affairs, Inc., Washington, D.C. (1992), p. 2.

[56] Ibid.

while the public's toleration of pollution decreases. Inevitably, these confrontations will be presented for a political solution inasmuch as no other mechanism for resolving such issues exists.[57]

One obvious byproduct of this political nature is delay; for example, the political debate over amending the Clean Air Act delayed the legislative process for almost 10 years. Similarly, air pollution regulations have repeatedly been slowed by political issues. While these delays are bemoaned by those who would like quicker action, they result from the need to resolve competing positions.[58]

Perhaps the basic reason that air pollution figures so prominently as a political consideration is its emotional impact. Like many other environmental issues, clean air is an extremely emotional matter, with people especially concerned about health impacts. Individuals who are exposed to or believe they have been exposed to carcinogenic chemicals have heightened worries. To a lesser extent, people become emotional as a result of concerns about the impact of air pollution on the environment. For example, the impact of acid rain on mountain lakes, orange-colored air in cities, and other serious environmental conditions resulting from air pollution provokes strong reactions. Emotions are also aroused when people feel financially threatened by

---

[57] Timothy A. Vanderver, Jr. et al., Clean Air Law and Regulation, The Bureau of National Affairs, Inc., Washington, D.C. (1992), pp. 2-3.

[58] Ibid., p. 3.

environmental regulations.[59]

Ideology and perceptions of our political system also play a significant role in the politics of air pollution. Some environmental groups and environmental activists appear to have concerns beyond the environment and clean air, such as opposition to the way the system presently works. As a result, at times, there may be suspicions that some groups are using environmental issues in an attempt to effect broader changes in society.[60]

Nor is ideology confined to environmentalists, since those who sometimes oppose environmental regulations also bring their own beliefs to the fray. Respect for the rights of private property, the profit motive, and concerns for the economic needs of the country are generally the basic reference points of these groups. In addition, there is often a reaction to the suspected agenda of the other side.[61]

Closely related to ideology and perceptions of our system are players' perceptions of other players in the clean air scenario. Environmentalists see their opponents as greedy and exploitative. The other side sees environmentalists and environmental groups as unrealistic, elitist, and perhaps out to change the world, using environmental issues as their weapon. These respective views are usually projected upon the Environmental Protection Agency

---

[59] Timothy A. Vanderver, Jr. et al., Clean Air Law and Regulation, The Bureau of National Affairs, Inc., Washington, D.C. (1992), p. 3.

[60] Ibid.

[61] Ibid.

(EPA), depending upon the player's views of the Agency and of the Agency's most recent actions.[62]

This congeries of human actions and reactions promises an interesting and complex process, a promise that has been amply fulfilled. The result has been to further complicate an already complex clean air field.[63]

Issues Broadly Affecting the Clean Air Program

A. Health as a Driving Force

Human health is the driving force behind air pollution regulation. For example, over the centuries, the impact on human health and the fatalities resulting from the uncontrolled burning of coal have been enormous. Other air pollutants similarly have significant health impacts. Thus, the primary objective of clean air regulation should be promoting standards which protect human health.[64]

One problem is that this objective has not always been clearly expressed. Too often, legitimate health concerns have been lost in the debate. In this context, it is encouraging to note that

---

[62] Timothy A. Vanderver, Jr. et al., Clean Air Law and Regulation, The Bureau of National Affairs, Inc., Washington, D.C. (1992), p. 3.

[63] Ibid.

[64] Timothy A. Vanderver, Jr. et al., Clean Air Law and Regulation, The Bureau of National Affairs, Inc., Washington, D.C. (1992), pp. 3-4.

the legislative debates leading to the 1990 Amendments focused primarily upon the health impacts of air pollution and the consequent need for legislative solutions.[65]

A second, more significant problem is the misuse of health concerns, both by proponents and opponents of more stringent regulation. The impact of air pollution upon human health, like many other scientific issues, is fraught with uncertainties and therefore subject to varying interpretations. Proponents of more stringent regulation are frequently accused of using health issues as a scare tactic to obtain their goals while opponents are generally perceived as down-playing health effects and emphasizing the inconclusive nature of current scientific knowledge. Neither is desirable but the uncertainties involved make this clash unavoidable.[66]

Some nonhealth concerns also are clearly legitimate bases for regulation. For example, most Americans strongly support requirements assuring pristine vistas from national parks. Nonetheless, while these objectives should receive appropriate consideration, they must be secondary. Human health protection should be the primary objective of air pollution regulation, until adverse health impacts are adequately controlled, and should be clearly recognized as the governing force.[67]

---

[65] Ibid., p. 4.

[66] Ibid.

[67] Timothy A. Vanderver, Jr. et al., Clean Air Law and Regulation, The Bureau of National Affairs, Inc., Washington, D.C. (1992), p. 4.

B. State/Federal Relationships

After decades of leaving air pollution issues to state and local governments, the federal government entered the picture. As is often the case with federal involvement, each subsequent federal effort increased the federal role, and ultimately resulted in federal dominance of air pollution regulation.[68]

The general statutory scheme established by the Clean Air Act has been for Congress and EPA to establish rules which the states are supposed to implement. States are supposed to utilize such tools as state implementation plans and state enforcement measures. Suitably Draconian penalties have been established for those states which fail to perform their designated role, although these penalties have proved politically difficult to apply.[69]

Not surprisingly, this scheme has caused resentment on the part of the states. In addition, it has created significant financial concerns since the federal government has tended to impose program requirements on the states without providing adequate funding. This concern may be ameliorated by the permit fee program established by the 1990 Amendments.[70]

Another state/federal issue concerns federal preemption of state laws. Under the Clean Air Act, the degree of preemption

---

[68] Ibid.

[69] Timothy A. Vanderver, Jr. et al., Clean Air Law and Regulation, The Bureau of National Affairs, Inc., Washington, D.C. (1992), p. 4.

[70] Ibid.

varies depending on the regulatory program (e.g., stationary sources generally, motor fuels, motor vehicles). States want the authority to enact and enforce their own laws, which may be more stringent than federal requirements. Industry generally opposes additional state requirements on the ground that a number of different laws with different requirements will necessitate differing methods of production, thus increasing the cost of producing and distributing various goods. This debate leads to efforts to resolve matters in the political arena. Political resolution, with respect to preemption as with respect to many other issues, often leads to unclear legislative mandates and consequently to further debate.[71]

A good example of the preemption issue involves states' ability to impose requirements on motor vehicles and motor vehicle fuels. Considerable uncertainty has existed on this subject and that debate continues.[72]

C. Transboundary Pollution

Air currents and pollutants flow across both state and national boundaries, thereby creating disputes about air pollution between states and nations. Clean Air Act § 126 governs disputes between states, and provides that a state may petition EPA for a finding that pollution from sources in another state is interfering with the petitioning state's efforts to meet or maintain air quality standards. Section 126 additionally requires a proposed new source of pollutants which may affect air quality in other states to

---

[71] Timothy A. Vanderver, Jr. et al., Clean Air Law and Regulation, The Bureau of National Affairs, Inc., Washington, D.C. (1992), pp. 4-5.

[72] Ibid., p. 5.

provide written notice to all nearby states at least 60 days before construction of the source is to commence. The actual prohibition against interstate pollution is contained in § 110, which prior to 1990 required state implementation plans to prohibit stationary sources in the state from emitting pollutants in amounts which would prevent achievement or maintenance of national air quality standards by another state.[73]

These pre-1990 provisions failed to adequately address interstate pollution problems, as those problems continue to exist and worsen today. Part of that ineffectiveness resulted from EPA's inability or unwillingness to take action under these provisions. In fact, EPA promulgated no regulations under these provisions and took no action against any sources of interstate pollution from the time they were enacted in 1977.[74] Further, the statutory language was uncertain in scope and meaning in a number of respects. This uncertainty resulted in judicial decisions that attempted to allocate the burden fairly among those sources who "significantly contributed" to interstate pollution, but that had the practical effect of affirming the denial of almost all § 126 petitions.[75]

The 1990 Amendments, while leaving § 126 virtually unchanged, revise the language in § 110, which now prohibits any

---

[73] Clean Air Act [hereinafter CAA], § 110(a)(2)(E), 42 U.S.C. § 7410(a)(2)(E) (1977).

[74] See *New York v. EPA*, 852 F.2d 574, 581 (D.C. Cir. 1988).

[75] See *Connecticut v. EPA*, 696 F.2d 147, 162-67 (2d Cir. 1982); *Jefferson County v. EPA*, 739 F.2d 1071, at 1088-94 (6th Cir. 1984).

source or other type of emissions activity within the state from emitting air pollutants that will contribute significantly to nonattainment or interfere with maintenance of ambient air standards by another state.[76] This language codifies the "significant contribution" approach courts had taken previously, and includes mobile sources in the prohibition against interstate pollution. These changes at least acknowledge the importance of equally sharing the burden for interstate pollution among all contributing sources. The 1990 Amendments also include acid rain provisions, which should affect many existing transboundary pollution problems.[77]

The 1990 Amendments additionally include several provisions which specifically address interstate problems in nonattainment areas.[78] Section 176A authorizes EPA to establish interstate transport regions and transport commissions where it finds that pollution from one or more states contributes significantly to violation of air quality standards in one or more other states. Section 184 establishes by law a transport region for ozone among the northeastern states, and requires that each state's implementation plan contain certain control measures, as well as providing a procedure for the commission to recommend additional

---

[76] CAA § 110(a)(2)(D), 42 U.S.C. § 7410(a)(2)(D) (1990).

[77] Timothy A. Vanderver, Jr. et al., Clean Air Law and Regulation, The Bureau of National Affairs, Inc., Washington, D.C. (1992), pp. 5-6.

[78] CAA §§ 176A and 184, 42 U.S.C. §§ 7506a and 7511c (1990).

control measures.[79]

When pollution crosses national boundaries, it becomes an international issue. Canada was extremely active in the U.S. acid rain debate in the 1980s because of its belief that emissions from the U.S. midwest were affecting Canada. It attempted to compel regulation of acid rain precursors through litigation, although such efforts ultimately proved unsuccessful.[80] Its political efforts were more successful as acid rain legislation eventually became a major component of the 1990 Amendments. Even with respect to the Amendments, however, it may be that Canada's concerns were used by U.S. players as a means of bolstering their own positions.[81]

The obverse of Canada's concerns relates to air pollution from Mexico. The predominant air flow is from that nation to the United States, which has raised concerns about air pollution from Mexican industry coming into the United States. These concerns have been exacerbated by the "maquiladora," facilities that are owned by U.S. companies and that are located just across the

---

[79] Timothy A. Vanderver, Jr. et al., Clean Air Law and Regulation, The Bureau of National Affairs, Inc., Washington, D.C. (1992), p. 6.

[80] See *Thomas v. New York*, 802 F.2d 1443 (D.C. Cir. 1986), *cert. denied*, 482 U.S. 919, 107 S.Ct. 3196, 96 L.Ed.2d 684 (1987); *Her Majesty the Queen in Right of Ontario v. U.S. EPA*, 912 F.2d 1525 (D.C. Cir. 1990).

[81] Timothy A. Vanderver, Jr. et al., Clean Air Law and Regulation, The Bureau of National Affairs, Inc., Washington, D.C. (1992), p. 6.

border. Maquiladora raise interesting issues concerning the export of pollution, especially since it can be argued that the pollution was originally exported by the United States and later re-exported by Mexico. The Mexico-to-U.S. air pollution issue is one to be primarily resolved by diplomacy, and the growing significance of environmental issues in diplomatic relations was highlighted by the role that transboundary pollution played at the November 1990 meeting between the presidents of the two countries.[82]

D. The Technology-Forcing Nature of the Act

In enacting the Clean Air Act, Congress deliberately chose a technology-forcing strategy, which embodies a policy that polluters must invent (if necessary) the necessary control technology to meet applicable emission standards or close down. The Supreme Court explicitly recognized the technology-forcing approach of the 1970 Amendments in the *Union Electric* case, holding that technological or economic infeasibility was not a legitimate basis for setting aside a state implementation plan which was otherwise sufficient to attain the national ambient air quality standards.[83] The Court found that Congress intended to produce significant improvements in air pollution control, and sources would have to comply with stringent state emission control

---

[82] Timothy A. Vanderver, Jr. et al., Clean Air Law and Regulation, The Bureau of National Affairs, Inc., Washington, D.C. (1992), p. 6.

[83] *Union Electric Co. v. EPA*, 427 U.S. 246, 96 S.Ct. 2518, 49 L.Ed.2d 474 (1976).

requirements even if technologically impossible to achieve.[84]

The Court also provided some additional guidance in this area of the law. In the case of *Union Electric Co. v. EPA*,[85] Justice Marshall writing for a unanimous Court said:

> "After reviewing the relevant provision of the Clean Air Act Amendments of 1970 and their legislative history, we agree that Congress intended claims of economic and technological infeasibility to be wholly foreign to the Administrator's consideration of a state implementation plan.
>
> "These requirements are of a technology-forcing character and are expressly designed to force regulated sources to develop pollution control devices that might at the time appear to be economically or technologically infeasible.
>
> "This approach is apparent on the face of § 110 (a) (2). The provision sets out eight criteria that an implementation plan must satisfy, and provides that if these criteria are met and if the plan was adopted after reasonable notice and hearing, the Administrator 'shall approve' the proposed state plan. The mandatory 'shall' makes it quite clear that the Administrator is not to be concerned with factors other than those specified, and none of the eight factors appears to permit

---

[84] *Union Electric Co. v. EPA*, 427 U.S. 257, 96 S.Ct. 2518, 49 L.Ed.2d 474 (1976).

[85] 8 ERC 2143 (U.S. Sup.Ct. 1976).

consideration of technological or economic infeasibility."[86]

However, the opinion continues by setting forth that claims of infeasibility can be relevant. This infeasibility issue should be raised before the particular state agency while formulating the SIP. If the industry is not exempted in the original plan, then a variance may be submitted as a revision to the SIP. An industry denied exemption may take its claim of infeasibility to the state courts. Also, a state Governor may request an extension or postponement based on infeasibility grounds. Finally, claims of technological or economic feasibility are relevant to fashioning an appropriate compliance order between EPA and the operator in controversies arising under the Clean Air Act.[87]

This approach has been employed in the Act throughout its history. For example, the 1977 Amendments codified the requirements for prevention of significant deterioration, which require new sources that wish to locate in areas where air is cleaner than the national standards to employ the best available control technology, and further limit permissible degradation of air in those areas beyond what is required by national ambient air standards.[88] These provisions employ technology-forcing by

---

[86] Environmental Law Handbook, J. Gordon Arbuckle, G. William Frick, Marshall Lee Miller, Thomas F.P. Sullivan and Timothy A. Vanderver, Jr., (September 1979, Sixth Edition), pp. 37-38.

[87] Ibid., p. 38.

[88] CAA §§ 163(b), 165(a)(4)(d), 42 U.S.C. §§ 7473(b), 7475(a)(4)(d) (1977).

making industrial expansion contingent upon the development of better emission controls, and requiring each new source to incorporate the latest technological improvements.[89]

Similarly, the 1990 Amendments contain pollutant-specific nonattainment provisions which include stringent control requirements on new stationary sources locating in nonattainment areas, and provide that new sources of most pollutants may not be built without net emissions reductions of those pollutants by existing sources.[90] These provisions demonstrate that technology-forcing continues to be a driving strategy in the Clean Air Act.[91]

This approach, while enduring, has been the object of much controversy. It has been criticized as unrealistic, unfair, and, most important, ineffective in producing innovation. Others credit technology-forcing under the Clean Air Act with the development of important air pollution control technologies such as "scrubbers," a sulfur dioxide control technology developed and used by the electric power industry.[92] Regardless of one's point of view concerning the effectiveness of technology-forcing, it is an aspect

---

[89] Timothy A. Vanderver, Jr. et al., Clean Air Law and Regulation, The Bureau of National Affairs, Inc., Washington, D.C. (1992), p. 7.

[90] See, e.g., the ozone nonattainment provisions in §§ 181-85.

[91] Timothy A. Vanderver, Jr. et al., Clean Air Law and Regulation, The Bureau of National Affairs, Inc., Washington, D.C. (1992), p. 7.

[92] Note, Forcing Technology: The Clean Air Act Experience, 88 Yale L.J.1713, 1722-30 (1979).

of clean air regulation which industry will have to continue to take into account.[93]

E. No Air Permit Program Before 1990

Originally, operating permits were not required by the Clean Air Act although state and/or local governments often required construction and operating permits for sources of air pollution. Instead, the pre-1990 Act utilized the State Implementation Plan (SIP) mechanism in lieu of a permit program. The SIP is developed by the appropriate state authority to assure, for a given area within the state, the attainment or maintenance of federal air quality standards. It sets forth permissible emission limits for various categories of stationary sources, monitoring requirements, and other directives necessary for the regulation of air pollution.[94]

The SIP approach has the advantage of establishing across-the-board requirements, thereby enabling the program to be administered with less effort than would be required for a permit program. On the other hand, the SIP approach makes it more difficult to determine compliance, since there is no permit requirement for extensive reporting of emissions. This contrasts with the Clean Water Act approach, where extensive sampling and reporting requirements in permits have proved to be a principal

---

[93] Timothy A. Vanderver, Jr. et al., Clean Air Law and Regulation, The Bureau of National Affairs, Inc., Washington, D.C. (1992), p. 7.

[94] Timothy A. Vanderver, Jr. et al., Clean Air Law and Regulation, The Bureau of National Affairs, Inc., Washington, D.C. (1992), pp. 7-8.

source of evidence for enforcement actions. Also, under the SIP program, there have been disputes over the limits that are applicable to emissions from given industrial processes. Such disputes would not arise in the enforcement context if limits were set forth in a permit. Another negative is that a source's change in operations often requires a SIP revision. Since a SIP revision requires state rulemaking and EPA review, it is a clumsy way of dealing with operational changes.[95]

The 1990 Amendments require states to issue permits to virtually all sources. This should bring about a significant change in program implementation. Nonetheless, the effects of 20 years of using the SIP process in lieu of a permit program will linger for some time.[96]

F. What Is a Source?

Sources of pollutants regulated under the Clean Air Act include both stationary sources, typically industrial facilities such as power plants, and mobile sources, typically automobiles and trucks. The definition of "mobile sources" is fairly straightforward, with emissions and fuel requirements applicable to each individual vehicle. The definition of "stationary sources" provided in the Act is much less precise, however, and includes "any building, structure, facility, or installation which emits or

---

[95] Timothy A. Vanderver, Jr. et al., Clean Air Law and Regulation, The Bureau of National Affairs, Inc., Washington, D.C. (1992), p. 8.

[96] Ibid.

may emit any air pollutant."[97] The effort to define "source" in a completely comprehensive manner unfortunately has resulted in uncertainty as to what actually is the source that is to be regulated. This uncertainty has provided an opportunity for both industry and environmentalists to push for either a broader or narrower definition of a source, based on each group's particular agenda.[98]

For example, environmentalists generally favor defining the terms "facility" or "structure" very narrowly, so that each activity within an industrial complex which emits a pollutant would have to meet the applicable emissions standards. This would result in very rigid emissions controls and arguably the strictest regulation of air pollution. On the other hand, industry generally favors a broad definition of "source," so that one "facility" would include all activities which contribute to overall emissions by emitting one or several regulated pollutants. This definition would allow greater flexibility in meeting emissions limitations.[99]

The broader approach to defining "stationary sources" has been utilized by certain provisions of the Clean Air Act regulations, which further define the term "facility" in the definition of "stationary source" to include "all of the pollutant-emitting activities which belong to the same industrial grouping, or are located on contiguous properties, or are under the control

---

[97] CAA § 111(a)(3), 42 U.S.C. § 7411(a)(3) (1983); See also 40 C.F.R. pt. 52.01 (SIP approval and promulgation).

[98] Timothy A. Vanderver, Jr. et al., Clean Air Law and Regulation, The Bureau of National Affairs, Inc., Washington, D.C. (1992), p. 8.

[99] Ibid.

of the same person."[100] This reflects EPA's policy to allow states to use the most cost-effective measures to meet emissions limitations in their implementation plans, and is often referred to as the "bubble policy."[101]

The stringent requirements imposed by the 1990 Amendments on new and modified sources, as well as the additional controls required for many existing sources, make it likely that the regulated community will continue to support a broad definition of "stationary source," and that EPA will continue use of the bubble concept in as many circumstances as possible. The conflicting pressures created by this situation ensure that the definition of a "source" will continue to be a matter of debate.[102]

G. Stationary and Mobile Sources

There has always been the potential for mobile and stationary sources being pitted against one another. If only so much pollution will be tolerated, the "available" emissions have to be divided in some fashion among all sources. Who gets what share then becomes an issue, but this was not significant before 1990. In a sense, the issue of mobile source versus stationary source is a subset of a number of potential battles between sources: major sources v. major sources; major sources v. smaller sources;

---

[100] 40 C.F.R. pt. 51.165(ii) (new source review); 40 C.F.R. pt. 52.21(b)(5) (prevention of significant deterioration).

[101] Timothy A. Vanderver, Jr. et al., Clean Air Law and Regulation, The Bureau of National Affairs, Inc., Washington, D.C. (1992), p. 9.

[102] Ibid.

manmade sources v. natural sources; and so forth.[103]

The 1990 Amendments noticeably sharpen this antagonism between sources. The Amendments renewed the emphasis on requiring states to bring their ambient air into compliance with national standards (the National Ambient Air Quality Standards or NAAQS) and to show progress in doing so. This increased stringency has focused attention on the amount of pollution that can be emitted and therefore has caused real conflict.[104]

A good example of this conflict is the debate over the "California car." Congress provided for two sets of requirements for automobiles: one prescribed by the federal government, and one for vehicle emission standards developed by the State of California. The Amendments also permit other states to require the California car, and efforts are now under way in several states to impose such a requirement. Proponents of these measures have couched their arguments in terms of reducing pollution in their state. It is apparent, however, that in a number of states a principal objective is to "reserve" the allowable pollution for stationary sources. This is not surprising as local industries--and local jobs--are far more popular in statehouses than are "Big Oil" and the automobile industry in far-off Detroit.[105]

---

[103] Timothy A. Vanderver, Jr. et al., Clean Air Law and Regulation, The Bureau of National Affairs, Inc., Washington, D.C. (1992), p. 9.

[104] Ibid.

[105] Timothy A. Vanderver, Jr. et al., Clean Air Law and Regulation, The Bureau of National Affairs, Inc., Washington, D.C. (1992), p. 9.

The clash between mobile and stationary sources will only worsen. Increasing population, the increasing number of vehicles, and the increasing number of sources will expand the potential for pollution. It is clear that the country is not willing to tolerate increased pollution and indeed expects decreases. This virtually guarantees conflict over "sharing" the air emissions that are allowed.[106]

H. Market Incentives

From the outset, the Clean Air Act has had the typical "command-and-control" approach of environmental statutes: EPA establishes prescriptive standards (commands) and attempts to compel compliance with those standards (control). The command-and-control approach has repeatedly been criticized as inefficient and has also been attacked on ideological grounds. The argument underlying these criticisms is that the government should restrict pollution, not tell people how to achieve the desired result.[107]

As a consequence, there has been a continuing effort to inject market incentives or mechanisms into the regulatory scheme. Such incentives have been discussed for many years and, with the 1977 Amendments, began to have some role. One example is the "bubble policy" in which an imaginary bubble is drawn over an entire facility and a limit established for that facility. Thus, the owner/operator can determine how best to control air emissions

---

[106] Ibid., p. 10.

[107] Timothy A. Vanderver, Jr. et al., Clean Air Law and Regulation, The Bureau of National Affairs, Inc., Washington, D.C. (1992), p. 10.

and most efficiently meet the regulatory limit.[108]

Similarly, EPA has been attempting to set penalties based on the economic benefits of noncompliance. Section 120 provides for assessment of noncompliance penalties for violations of emissions standards or limitations, compliance schedules, hazardous air pollutant emissions standards, or applicable NSPS (New Source Performance Standards). The regulations governing assessment of these penalties are located at 40 C.F.R. pt. 66, 40 C.F.R. pt. 66.1(a) and state:

> This penalty is designed to recover the economic advantage which might otherwise accrue to a source by reason of its failure to comply with air pollution control standards after receipt of a notice of noncompliance.[109]

Although this provision was upheld (in almost all respects) in *Duquesne Light Co. v. EPA,*[110] it has rarely proved to be a dominant feature in penalty calculations. Rather, economic benefit is usually one of a number of factors that are used to calculate a proposed penalty and that together form the basis for subsequent negotiations and/or judicial review. On the whole, the past 20 years have seen a very heavy reliance on the command-and-control

---

[108] Ibid.

[109] Timothy A. Vanderver, Jr. et al., Clean Air Law and Regulation, The Bureau of National Affairs, Inc., Washington, D.C. (1992), p. 10.

[110] 698 F.2d 456 (D.C. Cir. 1983).

approach.[111]

With the 1990 Amendments, the emphasis has shifted to a greater use of market-based incentives and other market mechanisms. This change reflects both a response to the increasing costs of air pollution control and a recognition that command-and-control may not be the most effective approach in many cases.[112]

Probably the best example of the use of the market approach is the new acid rain provisions of Title IV.[113] These provisions are designed to significantly reduce sulfur dioxide and nitrogen oxide emissions from electric utilities by the year 2000, through a program based on an emission allowance system. Under this system, each regulated source will receive a certain number of annual allowances to emit sulfur dioxide, based on the applicable emissions limit set by the statute. These annual emission allowances may then be used by the source, saved for use in future years, or sold or traded to other sources.[114] EPA is also required to withhold a certain number of allowances for direct sale and auction.[115] The expected result is that sources will buy and sell emissions allowances in the open market, which will encourage

---

[111] Timothy A. Vanderver, Jr. et al., Clean Air Law and Regulation, The Bureau of National Affairs, Inc., Washington, D.C. (1992), p. 10.

[112] Ibid.

[113] CAA §§ 401-16, 42 U.S.C. §§ 7651, 7651a-o (1990).

[114] CAA §§ 402-405, 42 U.S.C. §§ 7651a-d (1990).

[115] CAA § 416, 42 U.S.C. § 7651o (1990).

emissions reductions in the most efficient manner. Although the nitrogen oxide provisions appear to be more typically based on command-and-control regulation, it is clear that, as a whole, the acid rain program relies very heavily on market forces and economic incentives to assure compliance with stringent emission limitations.[116]

Other aspects of the 1990 Amendments similarly reflect a growing reliance on market incentives in the regulation of air pollution. For example, the revised hazardous air pollutant provisions include incentives or credits for early emissions reductions. Under those provisions, if a source achieves a 90 percent reduction in emissions of a hazardous air pollutant prior to the time an emission standard is proposed, EPA or the state is required to set an alternate emission limitation for that source reflecting that reduction, and deferring compliance with the actual standard for six years.[117]

The revised enforcement provisions in the 1990 Amendments are also influenced by market-based considerations, and require EPA and courts to consider a number of economic factors when assessing penalties for violation of the Act, including the size of the business, the economic impact of the penalty on the business, and the economic benefit of noncompliance.[118]

---

[116] Timothy A. Vanderver, Jr. et al., Clean Air Law and Regulation, The Bureau of National Affairs, Inc., Washington, D.C. (1992), p. 11.

[117] CAA § 112(i), 42 U.S.C. § 7412(i) (1990).

[118] CAA § 113(e), 42 U.S.C. § 7413(e) (1990).

These and other provisions reflect the increased use of the market approach in clean air regulation, and quite possibly a general trend in environmental legislation as well.[119]

I. Cost and Impacts

The cost of air pollution control is already enormous, with EPA estimating pre-1990 costs at over $25 billion a year. These costs will be dramatically increased by the 1990 Amendments, with some estimates of added costs exceeding $20 billion annually. Such estimates have been disputed, but there will clearly be very large costs imposed by the Amendments.[120]

These costs will have significant impacts on the American economy. For example, the oil, automotive, and electric power industries face dramatic changes in the ways they do business as a result of the Amendments' various mandates. These changes may force restructuring of whole industries; another possibility is substantially differing impacts on companies within a single industry.[121]

Another impact is the creation of tremendous business opportunities. The provision of environmental protection equipment and services has grown dramatically over the last few years, and this growth will continue for air pollution goods and

---

[119] Timothy A. Vanderver, Jr. et al., Clean Air Law and Regulation, The Bureau of National Affairs, Inc., Washington, D.C. (1992), p. 11.

[120] Ibid.

[121] Ibid., pp. 11-12.

services as a consequence of the new requirements.[122]

J. The 1990 Amendments

As might be expected after one of the most intense legislative battles in years, the 1990 Amendments will have a tremendous impact on industry, regulators, and the general public. The likely parameters of this impact have been analyzed in numerous books and articles and will only be discussed briefly here.[123]

On the stationary source side, there is a dramatic increase in the number of substances that will be regulated as almost 200 substances have been brought under the aegis of air toxics. More new and existing sources will be regulated as a consequence of lower emissions thresholds, and the increased number of regulated substances will also lead to an increase in regulated sources.[124]

The mobile source area will find the federal government (and the California government, for "California cars" and "California fuels") in a substantially more intrusive role. The formulation of fuels will increasingly be performed to meet government requirements, and a critical component of future

---

[122] Timothy A. Vandervér, Jr. et al., Clean Air Law and Regulation, The Bureau of National Affairs, Inc., Washington, D.C. (1992), p. 12.

[123] Ibid.

[124] Ibid.

vehicle development will be emissions reduction.[125]

Finally, industry will find more and more people looking over its shoulder. In some situations, such as nonattainment and air toxics programs, it will find more federal control. In other areas, there will be more state and local control. The new permitting requirements will probably mean that there is more federal, and state, and local control. In addition to increased government activity, the new enforcement provisions assure more citizen involvement. This adds to the list of players who will be scrutinizing industry's compliance efforts. This increased exposure to enforcement will be complemented by the significantly increased civil and criminal penalties provided by the 1990 Amendments.[126]

The end result will be more operating constraints and significant financial outlays. The statutory scheme that leads to this result is summarized briefly below.[127]

Overview of Clean Air Regulation

The extraordinarily political nature of clean air legislation is emphasized by the 10-year debate that was required for reauthorizing the Act. Even during the last 2 years, during which the bills which ultimately became the 1990 Amendments were

---

[125] Timothy A. Vanderver, Jr. et al., Clean Air Law and Regulation, The Bureau of National Affairs, Inc., Washington, D.C. (1992), p. 12.

[126] Ibid.

[127] Ibid.

being considered, political questions were usually supreme. Congressman Henry Waxman of California, Chairman of the House Subcommittee that considered the reauthorization legislation, describes the legislative battles and the compromises leading to enactment and provides a wide-ranging policy overview of the key provisions of the Amendments. Waxman also discusses five important cross-cutting themes of the Amendments: very specific and mandatory directives to EPA; the broad availability of citizen lawsuits; the pervasive reliance on technology-forcing to achieve the statutory health and environmental protection objectives; reliance, where possible, on market-based pollution control initiatives; and control of emissions from previously unregulated sources. Finally, he sizes up the 1990 Amendments in a unique comparison of its provisions to the legislative proposals of the prior decade.[128]

Laying aside the technology-forcing issue, air regulation is closely related to a number of scientific and technological issues. Unfortunately, science and technology are often as uncertain as the law. While lawyers and regulators are reasonably comfortable with uncertainty in their fields of expertise, they often have trouble dealing with similar uncertainty in areas, such as science and technology, with which they are not as familiar. Scientific and technological uncertainty, the underlying imprecision of data that appear precise, and other deviations from scientific "black-and-white" can be a significant problem if ignored by the legislator, the

---

[128] Timothy A. Vanderver, Jr. et al., Clean Air Law and Regulation, The Bureau of National Affairs, Inc., Washington, D.C. (1992), pp. 12-13.

regulator, or the regulated entity.[129]

Science and technology impacts on air pollution regulation in a number of ways. Perhaps the simplest is determining the effect of pollution on health and the environment. An example of debate on this score concerns acid rain. The proponents of sulfur dioxide (SO_2) emission controls contended that science had established that acid rain was having significant adverse effects, such as destroying lakes. Opponents of such legislation argued that there was no definitive scientific determination. Coincidentally, the debate included a major issue relevant to the concern about scientific precision and accuracy: the modeling of air and air pollution flows. While modeling appears to give a definite picture of what is happening in the real world, these results often depend upon the model used and the data entered into the model.[130]

Another example as to the real effect of pollution involves the question of whether perchloroethylene (PCE or perc) is an ozone precursor. This would seem to be a simple scientific question, readily susceptible to a straightforward scientific answer. However, EPA has wrestled with this question for 15 years, taking each side at various times. Indeed, its most recent position has been to take both sides simultaneously, concluding that while PCE is probably not an ozone precursor, the Agency will treat it as if

---

[129] Timothy A. Vanderver, Jr. et al., Clean Air Law and Regulation, The Bureau of National Affairs, Inc., Washington, D.C. (1992), p. 13.

[130] Timothy A. Vanderver, Jr. et al., Clean Air Law and Regulation, The Bureau of National Affairs, Inc., Washington, D.C. (1992), p. 13.

it were.[131]

Related questions involve what is a "safe" level of air pollution and the impacts of various levels of pollutants on the public health generally and on particular groups of individuals. In turn, this leads to efforts to assess risks, which creates a whole new area of uncertainty.[132]

Another area in which science and technology is critical is whether pollution can either be eliminated or reduced and the degree of reduction that can be obtained. This is a question of what is doable and how. However, if technology-forcing is the basis for regulation, regulations do not need to consider technological issues, since in this situation, technology becomes relevant only after the regulations are promulgated.[133]

Finally, there are questions as to the sampling and analysis of emissions of various pollutants from various sources. The end result of sampling is a series of apparently precise emission results. Again, however, this may be subject to variability and uncertainty.[134]

The foregoing are only a few of the numerous scientific and

---

[131] Ibid.

[132] Ibid.

[133] Timothy A. Vanderver, Jr. et al., Clean Air Law and Regulation, The Bureau of National Affairs, Inc., Washington, D.C. (1992), p. 13.

[134] Ibid., p. 14.

technological issues presented by clean air regulation.[135]

As noted above, the Clean Air Act divides regulation into two categories: the regulation of mobile sources and the regulation of stationary sources. Each type of regulation is briefly outlined below.[136]

A. Mobile Sources

This topic is divided into the regulation of vehicles and of fuels used in those vehicles. Vehicle regulation has developed over a number of years. While fuels regulation has been in place for many years, it was dramatically transformed by the 1990 Amendments.[137]

1. Mobile Source Fuels and Fuel Additives

A system of vehicular emissions controls virtually requires a corresponding system regulating mobile source fuels and fuel additives. This system was set forth in § 211 of the Act.[138]

Federal fuels regulation has covered a period of approximately 30 years and has been marked by a changing federal

---

[135] Ibid.

[136] Ibid.

[137] Timothy A. Vanderver, Jr. et al., Clean Air Law and Regulation, The Bureau of National Affairs, Inc., Washington, D.C. (1992), p. 14.

[138] Ibid.

role. The earliest legislation directed the government to encourage industry in developing pollution reducing fuels. This has changed to a series of regulatory initiatives, which have become increasingly more stringent.[139]

Before the 1990 Amendments, EPA had taken a number of significant steps concerning the regulation of fuels and fuel additives. Among these steps were registration requirements for fuels and fuel additives and a prohibition on the marketing of new fuels or fuel additives that were not substantially similar to fuel used for certification of motor vehicles.[140]

Even more significant were a number of fuels regulations that were developed over the years. These include regulations governing the lead content of gasoline, the volatility of gasoline, and the sulfur content of diesel fuel.[141]

In the 1990 Amendments, Congress built upon the regulations described above and added new requirements. First, EPA was directed to issue new regulations for reformulated gasoline for the worst ozone nonattainment areas. Similarly, oxygenated gasoline will be required in certain carbon monoxide nonattainment areas. These programs anticipate use of these new types of gasoline in conventional vehicles. Note that the states can

---

[139] Ibid.

[140] Timothy A. Vanderver, Jr. et al., Clean Air Law and Regulation, The Bureau of National Affairs, Inc., Washington, D.C. (1992), p. 14.

[141] Ibid.

expand the geographic coverage of these two programs.[142]

EPA was directed to establish clean fuel standards for application through a pilot program in California. There are also provisions concerning the fueling of certain vehicle fleets and new types of fuel requirements for "urban buses." These requirements contemplate the possibility of new vehicle technologies.[143]

The Act provides for a system of penalties for violations of § 211. Civil penalties were increased by the 1990 Amendments and an "economic benefit of the violation" penalty was added.[144]

There is less federal preemption with respect to fuels regulation than with respect to vehicles. To oversimplify, state and local regulation is preempted for any fuel or fuel additive where EPA has made an affirmative finding that no regulation is necessary or has issued a regulation addressing the fuel or fuel additive sought to be regulated. If EPA does not take either of these steps, there will probably be no federal preemption. Further, federal preemption does not preclude state or local regulation for other nonenvironmental purposes.[145]

2. Vehicles

---

[142] Ibid.

[143] Timothy A. Vanderver, Jr. et al., Clean Air Law and Regulation, The Bureau of National Affairs, Inc., Washington, D.C. (1992), pp. 14-15.

[144] Ibid., p. 15.

[145] Ibid.

The system of vehicular emissions regulation has evolved over the last 30 years. Unlike the rest of the Clean Air Act, this is essentially a federal government program. With the exception of California, the state's role in this program is extremely limited. Indeed, the sole exemption to federal preemption for other states is allowing those states to adopt California standards for vehicles. A special grant of authority to California should not be surprising since the federal program has, by and large, followed the California example. The regulatory program for vehicles has been marked by increasing stringency as air pollution standards have not been met while the number of vehicles and the number of vehicle miles traveled has increased.[146]

The centerpiece of vehicular emissions regulation is tailpipe standards--permissible emissions from a variety of new vehicles. These include cars, light-duty trucks, and heavy-duty trucks. There are also separate sets of standards that must be met after a vehicle has been driven for so many miles or for so many years. In addition, a number of ancillary requirements, such as emissions warranties and onboard diagnostics, complement tailpipe standards.[147]

The 1990 Amendments may also result in air toxics requirements on vehicles as well as on fuels and stationary sources. However, the Amendments require EPA to study and develop, in the next few years, necessary regulations governing emissions of air toxics from vehicles and fuels. This differs from

---

[146] Timothy A. Vanderver, Jr. et al., Clean Air Law and Regulation, The Bureau of National Affairs, Inc., Washington, D.C. (1992), p. 15.

[147] Ibid.

the treatment of such emissions from stationary sources, for which air toxics standards are largely specified by the statute.[148]

A number of other elements are required to round out the statutory scheme for vehicles. These include a system of penalties, testing and certification requirements, emissions warranties, and manufacturer recalls. There are also provisions concerning nonroad engines and vehicles.[149]

B. Stationary Sources

1. The Regulatory Framework

The Act establishes two kinds of national standards--called National Ambient Air Quality Standards (NAAQS)--that are designed to limit permissible concentrations of air pollutants. Primary NAAQS are supposed to protect human health and secondary NAAQS are public welfare protection measures. EPA establishes the primary and secondary NAAQS after preparing necessary analyses to determine appropriate ambient air levels for various pollutants; the NAAQS are supposed to be reviewed at specified intervals. EPA has promulgated primary NAAQS only for a total of 6 pollutants: sulfur dioxide (SO_2), ozone (O_3), carbon monoxide (CO), lead (Pb), nitrogen dioxide (NO_2) and particulate

---

[148] Timothy A. Vanderver, Jr. et al., Clean Air Law and Regulation, The Bureau of National Affairs, Inc., Washington, D.C. (1992), p. 15.

[149] Ibid.

matter (PM_{10}).[150]

State Implementation Plans are the vehicles by which NAAQS are supposed to be achieved. They are intended to assure that emissions in a given area do not exceed the national air quality standards. The SIP establishes requirements for sources in the implementation area, which requirements are developed to assure compliance with the national standards. The SIP also includes implementation, attainment, maintenance, and enforcement measures. Indeed, until the enactment of a permitting program in the 1990 Amendments, it was the only federally sanctioned enforcement mechanism.[151]

Those areas whose pollutants exceed national ambient standards have been designated as "nonattainment" areas. Under the 1977 Amendments, SIPs for nonattainment areas were to achieve compliance with any applicable NAAQS not later than 1982. The key feature of the nonattainment program is its requirement for a permit to construct and operate new or modified major sources in nonattainment areas. The statute threatened Draconian sanctions for failure to achieve attainment, but these have proved unenforceable in practice.[152]

---

[150] Timothy A. Vanderver, Jr. et al., Clean Air Law and Regulation, The Bureau of National Affairs, Inc., Washington, D.C. (1992), pp. 15-16.

[151] Ibid., p. 16.

[152] Timothy A. Vanderver, Jr. et al., Clean Air Law and Regulation, The Bureau of National Affairs, Inc., Washington, D.C. (1992), p. 16.

The 1990 Amendments made major changes to the nonattainment provisions but not to the basic framework. New deadlines were established; control mechanisms were required; contingency measures were required for areas that do not come into compliance in the future. Greater pollution "offsets" were required for new or modified sources.[153]

The flipside of nonattainment is compliance. For areas complying with applicable NAAQS, Congress has established the Prevention of Significant Deterioration (PSD) program. The objective of PSD is to protect areas having high quality air and to discourage the exportation of pollution from nonattainment areas to relatively clean ones. One particularly controversial aspect of the PSD program has been those provisions concerning "visibility related" air quality which are, for example, designed to assure vistas around national parks.[154]

The final element of the basic framework is New Source Performance Standards (NSPS). These standards impose more stringent regulation on new and modified sources on the theory that such sources can meet more stringent standards. The statutory standard for such new and modified sources is the best system of emission control that has been adequately demonstrated. As a result of the more stringent regulation, significant questions arise as to what constitutes a "new" or "modified" source. The NSPS program was changed only slightly by the 1990 Amendments.[155]

---

[153] Ibid.

[154] Ibid.

[155] Timothy A. Vanderver, Jr. et al., Clean Air Law and Regulation, The Bureau of National Affairs, Inc., Washington,

2. *Air Toxics*

The 1990 Amendments replaced an ineffectual system of regulating hazardous air pollutants with a much more stringent system in a completely rewritten § 112. Section 112 now specifies 189 pollutants that are to be regulated as air toxics. The technology-based standard is "maximum achievable control technology" (MACT), and the statute provides a schedule by which EPA is to promulgate specific MACT standards. Health-based standards may be required if MACT proves inadequate. This program is primarily for major sources, which is defined in § 112 as an emitter of 10 tons per year of any of the 189 substances, or 25 tons per year of any combination of substances. There is a separate, less stringent system of regulation provided for smaller sources--called area sources.[156]

Section 112(r) establishes a program to control the accidental release of extremely hazardous substances, which are listed in that subsection. Sources emitting such extremely hazardous substances are required to develop a comprehensive risk management plan and move to correct potential hazards identified in the plan. An investigatory board was created to ascertain the causes of accidental releases.[157]

3. *Acid Rain*

D.C. (1992), p. 16.

[156] Timothy A. Vanderver, Jr. et al., Clean Air Law and Regulation, The Bureau of National Affairs, Inc., Washington, D.C. (1992), pp. 16-17.

[157] Ibid., p. 17.

Acid rain was one of the more controversial issues in the decade-long battle over reauthorizing the Act. The 1990 Amendments establish an entirely new program for control of acid rain, capping the gross quantities of sulfur dioxide (SO_2) emitted racheting down (NO_x) emissions. This program is based on a requirement that utility sources of SO_2 possess an "allowance" for each source of SO_2 emitted annually. This requirement is complemented by a system for trading these allowances and for saving them for later use.[158]

Two controversial issues on which EPA has not yet weighed in are the statutory provision allowing SO_2 emission sources not regulated by Title IV (i.e., industrial boilers) to opt into the acid rain program and receive saleable allowances, and EPA was directed to develop a program which will lead to a two million ton per year reduction in NO_x emissions below 1980 levels.[159]

4. *Stratospheric Ozone Protection*

Before the 1990 Amendments, the Clean Air Act contained only limited provisions concerning stratospheric ozone depletion. In 1987, the United States and most other industrial nations signed the Montreal Protocol on Substances that Deplete the Ozone Layer which was designed to freeze production levels of chlorofluorocarbons (CFCs) and then gradually reduce them

---

[158] Ibid.

[159] Timothy A. Vanderver, Jr. et al., Clean Air Law and Regulation, The Bureau of National Affairs, Inc., Washington, D.C. (1992), p. 17.

thereafter.[160]

Despite this international regime, Congress enacted, in Title VI of the 1990 Amendments, a new regulatory program. The Title VI program goes far beyond the requirements of the Montreal Protocol. It specifies certain substances to be listed as ozone-depleting substances and provides for the addition to these lists of other such substances. CFCs, halons, methly chloroform, and carbon tetrachloride are required to be phased out completely by the year 2000 (2002 for methyl chloroform, except for essential uses). Hydrochlorofluorocarbons (HCFCs), the first generation CFC substitutes, are also placed on a phase-out schedule.[161]

Title VI also imposes various monitoring and reporting requirements for ozone-depleting substances. It establishes special requirements for the servicing of motor vehicle air conditioners, a major source of ozone-depleting emissions. Labeling requirements for ozone-depleting substances are required. Perhaps most significantly, it requires EPA to develop a safe alternatives program to assess substitutes for ozone-depleting substances.[162]

5. *Permits*

The new permit program for stationary sources, which was created by the 1990 Amendments, covers virtually all major

---

[160] Ibid.

[161] Timothy A. Vanderver, Jr. et al., Clean Air Law and Regulation, The Bureau of National Affairs, Inc., Washington, D.C. (1992), pp. 17-18.

[162] Ibid., p. 18.

sources, as well as area sources. It will impact virtually all affected sources since it will assure greater public scrutiny and more effective enforcement.[163]

Like many other aspects of the Clean Air Act, the permit program divides labor and responsibility between the federal and state governments. The permit program will be state-run with federally specified elements. In addition, EPA is given specified functions in the permitting process. One noteworthy required feature is yearly emission fees for permit holders and applicants. In addition to the federally mandated requirements, states can have additional permit requirements.[164]

6. *Enforcement and Judicial Review*

The Act provides for both civil and criminal enforcement. Civil enforcement can be carried out either through administrative orders, including administrative penalty orders, or through judicial actions. The 1990 Amendments significantly increased enforcement authority, including substantial increases in penalties. As with most other aspects of the Clean Air Act program, federal/state issues frequently arise in the enforcement context.[165]

The 1990 Amendments criminalized a broad range of conduct. In view of the activities which may now lead to criminal

---

[163] Ibid.

[164] Timothy A. Vanderver, Jr. et al., Clean Air Law and Regulation, The Bureau of National Affairs, Inc., Washington, D.C. (1992), p. 18.

[165] Ibid.

prosecution, sources ought to have substantial concern about this aspect of enforcement.[166]

Congress also provided for citizen's suits--enforcement of the Act by "interested" citizens, who are typically environmental groups. The basis for such suits is the violation by a source of an "emission standard or limitation." The ability of citizens to sue for violations of permits and SIPs dramatically increases the enforcement pressure on sources.[167]

One defense attempted against new statutory and regulatory prescriptions has been to attack them on the grounds of vagueness. However, the courts have not been responsive to this argument in recent pollution cases.[168]

In *Houston Compressed Steel v. Texas*,[169] the Texas Clean Air Act's broad definition of "air pollution" was upheld by the Texas Court of Civil Appeals as not to be too vague to be employed against a scrap metal company that burned railroad boxcars outdoors. The opinion stated that "since the science of air

---

[166] Ibid.

[167] Timothy A. Vanderver, Jr. et al., Clean Air Law and Regulation, The Bureau of National Affairs, Inc., Washington, D.C. (1992), p. 18.

[168] Environmental Law Handbook, J. Gordon Arbuckle, G. William Frick, Marshall Lee Miller, Thomas F.P. Sullivan and Timothy A. Vanderver, Jr., (September 1979, Sixth Edition), p. 36.

[169] 456 S.W. 2d 768 (1970).

pollution control is new and inexact, and these standards are difficult to devise, if they are to be effective, they must be broad." The Texas Court also felt that an air polluter should not escape the consequences of his act merely because he is able to make his contaminants difficult to manage or control.[170]

In *Air Commission v. Coated Materials*,[171] the Pennsylvania Air Pollution Control Act's definition of air pollution, as some substance "which unreasonably interferes with the comfortable enjoyment of life and property" was founded to be uncertain, and was susceptible to acceptable standards of proof "since the language employed in the statute is equivalent to the definition of nuisance which is certainly established in the law."[172]

Similarly, the Connecticut General Statutes were found not unconstitutionally vague when they required every motor vehicle to be so equipped and adjusted as to prevent excessive fumes or exhaust smoke, since any ordinary and interested person would have no difficulty in determining whether or not a motor vehicle

---

[170] Environmental Law Handbook, J. Gordon Arbuckle, G. William Frick, Marshall Lee Miller, Thomas F.P. Sullivan and Timothy A. Vanderver, Jr., (September 1979, Sixth Edition), p. 36.

[171] 778 C.D. 1969 (Pa. Ct. Com. Pls. 1970).

[172] Environmental Law Handbook, J. Gordon Arbuckle, G. William Frick, Marshall Lee Miller, Thomas F.P. Sullivan and Timothy A. Vanderver, Jr., (September 1979, Sixth Edition), p. 36.

put out offensive or excessive fumes.[173]

Based on review of the case law, the argument of vagueness as a potential defense does not appear to offer a high probability for success.[174]

However, the availability of the defense of economic and technological infeasibility in cases arising under the Clean Air Act resulted in contrary or partially contrary decisions in the Federal Circuit Courts. So, the question was resolved by the Supreme Court. The question in issue was: Is technological or economic feasibility a defense against compliance with a State Implementation Plan (SIP) for air pollution control?[175]

What decisions an administrative agency makes depends on the statute. It is common for a Federal agency to have power to issue a cease and desist order, and in many instances an agency has the power to take affirmative action. An administrative order cannot be enforced in a court without an express provision in the statute.[176]

---

[173] *Connecticut v. Schuster's Express*, 6 Conn. Cir. Ct. 108 (1970).

[174] Environmental Law Handbook, J. Gordon Arbuckle, G. William Frick, Marshall Lee Miller, Thomas F.P. Sullivan and Timothy A. Vanderver, Jr., (September 1979, Sixth Edition), p. 36.

[175] Ibid., p. 37.

[176] Environmental Law Handbook, J. Gordon Arbuckle, G. William Frick, Marshall Lee Miller, Thomas F.P. Sullivan and

Generally, before a person is able to have a court review an administrative action, he must exhaust all his administrative remedies because courts are normally reluctant to interfere with administrative action before it is completed. Once the administrative remedies have been exhausted, then the matter is considered "ripe" for judicial review.[177]

Theoretically, the courts will not review the facts in the case but limit themselves to questions of law, or whether there has been abuse of authority and disregard of due process.[178]

Recent cases are worthy of examination because basic concepts are being challenged in this area of administrative law as the trend develops for the courts to interject themselves more and more into examining the operation of administrative agencies.[179]

On the state level in a case before the Pennsylvania Court of Common Pleas of Dauphin County, there was a challenge of the findings of the Pennsylvania Air Pollution Commission that a coil coating plant emitted odorous gases in violation of the state Air Pollution Control Act. The Court said that it could not modify the

---

Timothy A. Vanderver, Jr., (September 1979, Sixth Edition), p. 48.

[177] Ibid.

[178] Ibid.

[179] Ibid.

finding on the ground of credibility of evidence.[180] The Court said it only considered whether the Air Pollution Commission was arbitrary, and left credibility of the evidence to the Commission. This limited review is the usual approach taken by a court when considering an appeal from an administrative agency.[181]

REGULATION AND THE COURTS: THE CASE OF THE CLEAN AIR ACT[182]

Air Pollution Regulation, 1970-80

The air program is probably the most intellectually thin program we've got and it is the most overbuilt in terms of the law and the structure and the size ... That's a program that really has a church history problem. Every single congressional battle and staff battle is relevant to understanding why you're at the point you are now.

-EPA Administrator Douglas Costle

---

[180] *Air Commission v. Coated Materials*, 778 C.D. 1969 (Pa. Ct. Comm. Pls. 1970).

[181] Environmental Law Handbook, J. Gordon Arbuckle, G. William Frick, Marshall Lee Miller, Thomas F.P. Sullivan and Timothy A. Vanderver, Jr., (September 1979, Sixth Edition), p. 49.

[182] R. Shep Melnick, Regulation and the Courts: The Case of the Clean Air Act, The Brookings Institution, Washington, D.C. (1983), p. 24.

When President Ronald Reagan took office in 1981, many environmentalists feared his administration would convince Congress to weaken the Clean Air Act, the flagship of the environmental protection fleet. Reducing the burden of federal regulation was a major plank in Reagan's platform, and much of his criticism was aimed at environmental regulation. To make matters worse, the Act's authorization ran out in 1981, necessitating some form of congressional action. The Senate, which in the past had strongly supported the Act, was now in Republican hands. Especially after Reagan's surprising legislative victories on the budget and taxes, major revision of the Act seemed near.[183]

In December 1982, though, proposed amendments to the Act died quietly in committee. The House committee remained internally divided. Legislation supported by the Senate committee was unacceptable to the White House. Some observers doubt that a major revision of the Clean Air Act will become law before the 1984 presidential election.[184]

What is most striking about this sequence of events is not the failure of the Reagan administration to produce quick, major changes in the Act, but the similarities between 1981-82 and two prior periods, 1973-74 and 1976-77. In 1973, after the Arab oil embargo, President Richard M. Nixon proposed emergency energy legislation that would relax key provisions of the Clean Air Act. Despite calls for action to meet the energy crisis, Congress did not

---

[183] R. Shep Melnick, Regulation and the Courts: The Case of the Clean Air Act, The Brookings Institution, Washington, D.C. (1983), p. 24.

[184] Ibid.

pass a bill Nixon would sign until mid-1974. That legislation, the Energy Supply and Environmental Coordination Act,[185] contained few revisions of the Clean Air Act. The sponsors of the 1970 Act had successfully resisted retrenchment. In 1976 another Republican president, Gerald R. Ford, supported amendments to relax air pollution regulation, and Congress geared up for action. With inflation and unemployment running high and energy shortages on everyone's mind, environmentalists were once again on the defensive. Yet Congress did not produce amendments to the Act until 1977, and these amendments strengthened the Act in many ways.[186]

This brief history of clean air legislation emphasizes the continuities of environmental politics. While presidents--especially Republican ones--have favored relaxing regulatory demands, Congress has strengthened the Act more than it has weakened it. Air pollution regulation is so complex and controversial that Congress usually takes action a year or two after everyone announces that it "must" act "immediately." In the meantime other institutions--especially the Environmental Protection Agency, the states, and the courts--have tried to cope with the problems created by the Act.[187]

---

[185] 88 Stat. 258.

[186] R. Shep Melnick, Regulation and the Courts: The Case of the Clean Air Act, The Brookings Institution, Washington, D.C. (1983), pp. 24-25.

[187] R. Shep Melnick, Regulation and the Courts: The Case of the Clean Air Act, The Brookings Institution, Washington, D.C. (1983), p. 25.

1970: The Policy Breakthrough

Air pollution presents a classic example of a market externality or spillover. And the evolution of air pollution control in the United States provides an equally classic example of how the American political system typically handles such regulatory issues.[188] In the absence of government action, air pollution imposes costs on society in the form of adverse health effects, harm to vegetation and materials, and reduced visibility. Polluters, though, are seldom forced to compensate those who suffer this harm. As a result, those who use the air as a dumping ground fail to put a price on the consumption of a scarce natural resource--clean, breathable air. While it is generally conceded that government has a legitimate role to play in controlling such pollution, the federal government took almost no part in the process until the 1960s. Pollution control remained the domain of state and municipal public health agencies, which, with varying degrees of success, attempted to reduce the amount of visible pollution in the air of industrialized cities.[189]

---

[188] For a useful summary of the problem of externalities, see Stephen Breyer, Regulation and Its Reform (Harvard University Press, 1982). Two works that summarize the early history of pollution control are Richard B. Stewart and James E. Krier, Environmental Law and Policy, 2d ed. (Bobbs-Merrill, 1978); and James E. Krier and Edmund Ursin, Pollution and Policy: A Case Essay on California and Federal Experience with Motor Vehicle Air Pollution, 1940-1975 (University of California Press, 1977).

[189] R. Shep Melnick, Regulation and the Courts: The Case of the Clean Air Act, The Brookings Institution, Washington, D.C. (1983), p. 25.

Industrial growth after World War II produced increasing concern over air pollution. Utilities met growing demand for electricity by building coal-burning power plants that emitted large amounts of sulfur dioxide and particulate matter. In the late 1940s and early 1950s pollution from power plants and steel mills contributed to several "killer fogs" in Britain and the United States, causing thousands of premature deaths. Meanwhile, use of the automobile--which emits carbon monoxide, nitrogen oxides, and hydrocarbons--rose dramatically. Scientists investigating the origin of Los Angeles's famous smog discovered that the latter two pollutants interact to produce the brownish cloud that frequently caused eye irritation and various respiratory difficulties in residents of that city.[190]

States such as California, Pennsylvania, and New York took the lead in addressing these problems, and Congress took halting steps to help them (see *Major Provisions of Federal Legislation on Air Pollution Control* below). Federal involvement started in 1955 with small research projects and grants to the states. During the 1960s the federal government glided slowly, almost imperceptibly, into recommending safe pollution levels for various pollutants. The Air Quality Act of 1967 (the immediate predecessor of the legislation passed in the 1970s) charged the National Air Pollution Control Administration, a small unit within the Department of Health, Education and Welfare, with setting technologically feasible emission standards for new automobiles and helping the states devise pollution control programs. Yet progress in reducing pollution levels remained painfully slow. By 1969 most observers had labeled the federal program a nearly

---

[190] R. Shep Melnick, Regulation and the Courts: The Case of the Clean Air Act, The Brookings Institution, Washington, D.C. (1983), p. 26.

complete failure.[191]

MAJOR PROVISIONS OF FEDERAL LEGISLATION ON AIR POLLUTION CONTROL[192]

Major Provision: Air quality standards

Air Quality Act of 1967[193]

Set by states on basis of studies by federal government

Clean Air Act Amendments of 1970[194]

Uniform primary (health) and secondary (welfare) ambient air quality standards set by EPA.

---

[191] Richard J. Tobin, The Social Gamble: Determining Acceptable Levels of Air Quality (Lexington Books, 1979); J. Clarence Davies III and Barbara Davies, The Politics of Pollution, 2d ed. (Bobbs-Merrill, 1975).

[192] R. Shep Melnick, Regulation and the Courts: The Case of the Clean Air Act, The Brookings Institution, Washington, D.C. (1983), pp. 26-27.

[193] 81 Stat. 485; preceded by Air Pollution Control Act of 1955, 69 Stat. 322; Clean Air Act of 1963, 77 Stat. 392; and Motor Vehicle Air Pollution Control Act of 1965, 79 Stat. 992.

[194] 84 Stat. 1676.

Clean Air Act Amendments of 1977[195]

"Precautionary" nature of standards emphasized.

Major Provision: Attainment deadlines

Air Quality Act of 1967

None

Clean Air Act Amendments of 1970

Primary standards: 1975 or 1977 if extension granted.

Secondary: within reasonable time.

Clean Air Act Amendments of 1977

Primary: 1979 for stationary source pollutants; 1982 for mobile source pollutants or 1987 if extension granted.

Secondary: No change.

Major Provision: Implementation plans

Air Quality Act of 1967

States responsible for devising plans to meet air quality standards.

---

[195] 91 Stat. 685.

Clean Air Act Amendments of 1970

State implementation plans (SIPs) due in 1972; must include enforceable emission limitations and schedules; EPA must either approve or set alternative emission limits.

Clean Air Act Amendments of 1977

Systematic reassessment of SIPs for nonattainment areas required by 1979; prevention of significant deterioration (PSD) and offset programs expanded; limits placed on use of dispersion enhancement; special provisions for problem sources.

Major Provision: Enforcement

Air Quality Act of 1967

Left to states, except for cumbersome conference procedure.

Clean Air Act Amendments of 1970

Emission limitations enforceable by both state and federal government; criminal penalties and injunctions authorized; provision for citizen suits.

Clean Air Act Amendments of 1977

Civil penalties and noncompliance penalties added; construction ban and other sanctions for failing to attain air quality standards.

Major Provision: New Sources

Air Quality Act of 1967

No provisions.

Clean Air Act Amendments of 1970

Uniform new source performance standards (NSPS) set by EPA.

Clean Air Act Amendments of 1977

Attainment areas: best available control technology plus review of PSD increment consumption.

Nonattainment: lowest achievable emission rate plus offset review.

Coal-burning power plants: percentage reduction of sulfur in fuel.

Major Provision: Motor Vehicle Emissions

Air Quality Act of 1967

Federal government sets "feasible" emission standards for new vehicles.

Clean Air Act Amendments of 1970

New vehicles must reduce emissions to 90 percent of 1970 level no later than 1975-76.

Clean Air Act Amendments of 1977

Deadline for hydrocarbon and carbon monoxide standards extended; nitrogen oxides standard relaxed.

Major Provision: Transportation Controls

Air Quality Act of 1967

No provisions.

Clean Air Act Amendments of 1970

State plans must include "land-use and transportation controls" necessary to attain air quality standards.

Clean Air Act Amendments of 1977

Deadline for transportation controls extended; indirect source review made discretionary for states.

Major Provision: Judicial Review

Air Quality Act of 1967

Administrative Procedure Act governs.

Clean Air Act Amendments of 1970

Challenges of regulations in "appropriate circuit"; citizen suits in federal district court.

Clean Air Act Amendments of 1977

D.C. Circuit identified as "appropriate circuit" for regulations of national applicability.

The year 1970 was a political watershed for pollution control. The Earth Day activities of that spring called attention to the nation's many environmental problems. Politicians and the media claimed that air and water pollution were creating an environmental crisis. New organizations formed to promote environmental protection. President Nixon introduced a bill to strengthen air pollution legislation and later issued a reorganization plan creating the Environmental Protection Agency.[196] Senator Edmund S. Muskie, Democrat of Maine, the author of previous air pollution legislation and chairman of the Senate Subcommittee on Environmental Pollution, moved quickly to ensure that Nixon would neither receive political credit for jumping on the environmental protection bandwagon nor produce a new Act with more bark than bite. Not only had Muskie long advocated stronger pollution control measures, but he also expected to be running for president against Nixon in 1972. A 1970 report by Ralph Nader's Center for Study of Responsive Law charging Muskie with being soft on polluters strengthened the senator's resolve to push a tough bill through Congress.[197] After months of one-upmanship, Muskie succeeded in creating a very ambitious law.[198]

---

[196] 35 Fed. Reg. 15623 (1970).

[197] John C. Esposito, Vanishing Air (Grossman, 1970).

[198] Useful accounts of the passage of the 1970 Act include Charles O. Jones, Clean Air: The Policies and Politics of Pollution

The section of the 1970 Act that received most attention in Congress and the press was the requirement that by 1975 auto manufacturers reduce the emissions of new cars by 90 percent. Detroit and the Nixon administration claimed this was technologically infeasible. Senator Muskie responded that the 90 percent figure was based on estimates of the pollution reduction necessary to protect human health and that setting such federal standards would force the development of new technology. Thus was born the concept of "technology-forcing," which has since become a major theme of the Act.[199]

The sections of the Act involving stationary sources received much less attention in the press and on the House and Senate floor, but were no less sweeping. The Act required the EPA to set new source performance standards (NSPS) for all major categories of polluting facilities. Each standard was required to "reflect the degree of emission limitation achievable through the application of the best system of emission reduction which ... has been adequately demonstrated" (§ 111). The Administrator was also instructed to set emission limitations for "hazardous pollutants," to regulate fuel and fuel additives, and to

Control (University of Pittsburgh Press, 1975); Alfred Marcus, "Environmental Protection Agency," in James Q. Wilson, ed., The Politics of Regulation (Basic Books, 1980); and Helen Ingram, "The Political Rationality of Innovation: The Clean Air Act Amendments of 1970," in Ann F. Friedlaender, ed., Approaches to Controlling Air Pollution (MIT Press, 1978).

[199] John E. Bonine, "The Evolution of 'Technology-Forcing' in the Clean Air Act," *Environment Reporter*, Monograph 21 (Bureau of National Affairs, 1975); and Jones, Clean Air, chap. 7.

establish emission standards for aircraft.[200]

As important as these provisions were, the centerpiece of the 1970 Act was the national ambient air quality standards (NAAQS). The Act created a three-step process to define and achieve adequate air quality:

1. The EPA must set "primary" and "secondary" standards for all pollutants that "endanger the public health or welfare." Primary standards must be adequate to "protect the public health" by incorporating "an adequate margin of safety." Secondary standards must be adequate to "protect the public welfare from any known or anticipated adverse effects" (§§ 108 and 109).

2. States must submit by 1972 state implementation plans (SIPs) adequate to meet primary standards by 1975 and secondary standards within "a reasonable time." These SIPs must include "emission limitations, schedules, and timetables for compliance with such limitations, and such other measures as may be necessary to insure attainment and maintenance of such primary or secondary standard, including, but not limited to, land-use and transportation controls" (§ 110). If the EPA determines that all or part of a SIP is inadequate, it must promptly promulgate an adequate plan of its own.

---

[200] R. Shep Melnick, Regulation and the Courts: The Case of the Clean Air Act, The Brookings Institution, Washington, D.C. (1983), p. 29.

3. The requirements of each SIP are enforceable in both federal and state courts. The EPA can ask federal courts to impose criminal penalties for "knowing violators" of SIP rules or to issue injunctions stopping further violation (§ 113).[201]

The 1970 Act was far more detailed than most previous regulatory statutes. Most sections included deadlines for administrative action. Not only did the Act specify precise emission limitations for new cars, but the Senate report suggested exact numerical standards for several key pollutants. Yet much was left to administrative discretion. The need for discretion, coupled with congressional distrust of the Nixon administration, led the authors of the Act to include liberal judicial review provisions.[202]

Political scientists have noted that when the direct costs of regulation fall on a small, well-defined group (such as polluters) and benefits accrue to a large, dispersed collection of individuals (such as those who breathe the air), the former often come to dominate the administrative process once the initial enthusiasm for regulation dissipates.[203] Those who benefit from controls find it

---

[201] R. Shep Melnick, Regulation and the Courts: The Case of the Clean Air Act, The Brookings Institution, Washington, D.C. (1983), p. 29.

[202] Ibid., p. 30.

[203] Marver Bernstein, Regulating Business by Independent Commission (Princeton University Press, 1955), chap. 3; James Q. Wilson, "The Politics of Regulation," in James W. McKie, ed., Social Responsibility and the Business Predicament (Brookings

hard to organize lobbying efforts to counterbalance the ability of those being regulated to maintain a daily presence in the administrative process. As a result, victories achieved in a legislative breakthrough slowly evaporate as administrators develop a specific program to carry out statutory commands.[204]

Although the Environmental Protection Agency was not as brash or aggressive by 1980 as it was in the early 1970s, it maintained a strong sense of mission and an adversarial relation with industry throughout the decade. None but the most unrelenting environmentalist would claim (at least until the Reagan administration made its appointments in 1981) that polluters had "captured" the EPA.[205]

This is particularly surprising in light of the changing economic and political context of regulation. The 1960s and early 1970s were years of constant economic growth. Just as politicians looked for ways to spend the fiscal surplus, they expected business to be able to finance pollution control from its substantial profits. In the mid- and late 1970s, however, inflation, unemployment, and energy dominated political discourse. Many costly EPA regulations came into effect just as the nation was sliding into the

---

Institution, 1974); and Mancur Olson, Jr., The Logic of Collective Action (Harvard University Press, 1965).

[204] R. Shep Melnick, Regulation and the Courts: The Case of the Clean Air Act, The Brookings Institution, Washington, D.C. (1983), p. 30.

[205] R. Shep Melnick, Regulation and the Courts: The Case of the Clean Air Act, The Brookings Institution, Washington, D.C. (1983), p. 30.

recession of 1974-75. The EPA often received blame for fueling inflation and adding to the unemployment rolls. In addition, air pollution regulations that increased energy consumption (such as restrictions on the use of leaded gasoline) or that limited the use of domestic fuels (such as sulfur dioxide standards limiting the burning of coal) led to constant battles between the EPA and those whose primary concern was reducing American dependence on foreign oil. To see why large-scale administrative and legislative retreat did not occur in the 1970s one must look in greater detail first at the political coalition supporting regulation and then at the agency administering it.[206]

Political Actors and Coalitions

By imposing burdens on a wide variety of polluters and consumers and by promising benefits to an equally wide variety of groups and citizens, the Clean Air Act has drawn a multitude of participants into the debate over regulation of air pollution. On occasion these groups have formed strange coalitions. For example, in 1977 environmentalists united with eastern high-sulfur coal interests to impose further restrictions on low-sulfur western coal.[207] Yet coalitions on clean air issues have remained nearly constant since 1970. Environmentalist groups have received strong support from congressional committees, especially in the Senate. Industry has sought help from the White House, other federal agencies, and the states. Caught between its two masters, Congress and the president, the EPA has sided more often with the

---

[206] Ibid., pp. 30-31.

[207] Bruce A. Ackerman and William T. Hassler, Clean Coal/Dirty Air (Yale University Press, 1981).

former than the latter.[208]

Congress and the Executive

From the time he sponsored the Clean Air Acts of 1965, 1967, and 1970 until he left Congress to become Secretary of State, Senator Edmund S. Muskie was the political figure with the greatest influence on air pollution policy. With years of experience in the field, the respect to the vast majority of the Senate, the ability to command media attention, and an enviable capacity for outmaneuvering his opponents, Muskie controlled the tempo as well as the substance of congressional action. Time and again Muskie staved off attempts to amend the Act until the political environment was favorable to his cause. As chairman of the Subcommittee on Environmental Pollution of the Senate Committee on Public Works (later renamed the Committee on Environment and Public Works), Muskie held detailed annual oversight hearings on the implementation of the Act. He expected the EPA to consult with him or his staff on major policy decisions. Muskie made clear what he thought Congress had intended in 1970--especially when he believed the administration was pressuring the EPA to act differently.[209]

Senator Muskie had two sets of allies within the Senate.

---

[208] R. Shep Melnick, Regulation and the Courts: The Case of the Clean Air Act, The Brookings Institution, Washington, D.C. (1983), p. 31.

[209] Bernard Asbell chronicles many of Muskie's activities in The Senate Nobody Knows (Johns Hopkins University Press, 1978). This journalistic account provides an interesting view of Muskie's influence on the 1977 Amendments.

The first was a dedicated, aggressive, knowledgeable staff. Muskie aides, particularly Leon Billings, developed a reputation for both influence and arrogance. Without their assistance the Subcommittee on Environmental Pollution--which became known as "the Muskie committee"--would not have been able to write such detailed legislation and reports, conduct its many hearings, and keep abreast of daily activities at the EPA.[210]

The second set of allies was the Republicans on the subcommittee. Senator Muskie developed close working relations with those minority members who participated actively in policymaking for pollution control, including Howard Baker, Robert Stafford, Pete Domenici, John Chafee, and even the more conservative James Buckley. These senators, like their Democratic colleagues, chose to devote their attention to environmental issues because they believed that the federal government should take strong action to prevent environmental degradation. At times Republicans on the committee have offered stronger support for environmental programs than have Democrats. One of the ironies of the 1980 election, which brought the Senate under control of the Republicans, is that the two men who became chairmen of the full committee and the subcommittee--Robert Stafford and John Chafee--have resisted relaxation of the Act more vigorously than have their ranking Democratic counterparts.[211]

The House of Representatives did not play a major role in the writing of the 1970 Act, but has since steadily gained influence

---

[210] R. Shep Melnick, Regulation and the Courts: The Case of the Clean Air Act, The Brookings Institution, Washington, D.C. (1983), p. 32.

[211] Ibid.

over regulatory policy. The Clean Air Act falls within the jurisdiction of the Subcommittee on Health and the Environment of the House Energy and Commerce Committee. Until 1978 this subcommittee (which was one of the two busiest in the House) was chaired by Representative Paul G. Rogers, Democrat of Florida. While Senator Muskie was known as "Mr. Environment," Representative Rogers gained his reputation as "Mr. Health." His subcommittee treated the Act as a preventive health measure and sought to strengthen its health-related features.[212]

Rogers, like Muskie, assembled a young, competent, hard-driving staff, but he had trouble keeping committee members and the rest of the House in line. Rogers faced frequent challenges from Republicans in the subcommittee, Democrats in the full committee, and even other subcommittees--most notably the House Appropriations Committee's Subcommittee on Agriculture, Environmental and Consumer Protection, chaired until 1975 by the fiercely anti-EPA Jamie Whitten. In 1977 the Rogers subcommittee lost two key votes on the floor, the first on auto standards and the second on prevention of significant deterioration. When Rogers retired in 1978, a lively battle for the subcommittee chairmanship ensued. Henry Waxman of California, the most liberal of the candidates, eventually won. But his control over policymaking has been constantly challenged, especially by John Dingell of Michigan, the new chairman of the full committee. The difference between House and Senate reflects not just the personalities of legislative leaders, but also the greater skepticism about environmental programs expressed by the membership of the

---

[212] R. Shep Melnick, Regulation and the Courts: The Case of the Clean Air Act, The Brookings Institution, Washington, D.C. (1983), pp. 32-33.

lower House.[213]

Both the House and Senate subcommittees have frequently complained about presidential hostility to air pollution programs. This was particularly true during the Nixon administration. Despite the fact that Nixon created the EPA and signed some of the most ambitious environmental protection legislation in the country's history, he never received the trust of environmentalists in Congress or the loyalty of the EPA. Generally suspicious of the federal bureaucracy and concerned about the costs the Clean Air Act placed on industry, the president and his White House staff carefully reviewed activity in the EPA, sought to block many agency regulations, and introduced legislation to reduce the EPA's goals and authority. By 1974, antagonism between the Nixon administration and the EPA had become so great that Administrator Russell Train (recently appointed by Nixon) refused to support legislative revisions proposed by the White House and other federal agencies. The weakening of the presidency in the wake of Watergate strengthened the position of the EPA and congressional committees. As one insider put it, Train survived only "because Richard Nixon did not."[214]

---

[213] R. Shep Melnick, Regulation and the Courts: The Case of the Clean Air Act, The Brookings Institution, Washington, D.C. (1983), p. 33.

[214] Robert Sansom, The New American Dream Machine: Toward a Simpler Lifestyle in an Environmental Age (Doubleday, 1976), p. 25. Sansom was assistant administrator for air programs. Deputy Administrator John Quarles tells a similar story in Cleaning Up America: An Insider's View of the Environmental Protection Agency (Houghton Mifflin, 1976).

Hostility between Congress and the president and cool relations between the EPA and the White House continued under Gerald Ford. More surprising was the reemergence of this pattern under President Jimmy Carter. Carter received the support of environmental groups in the 1976 election, appointed several leaders of these organizations to top positions in the EPA, and endorsed much of the legislation developed by the Muskie and Rogers committees. Yet he, too, was eventually attacked by environmentalists for trying to water down EPA rules and was criticized in special hearings of the Muskie committee for "interfering" with air pollution regulation.[215] However, President Reagan's appointment of many political executives with close ties to industry and his major cuts in the EPA's budget have made many environmentalists and congressmen look upon his predecessor more positively.[216]

What accounts for the constant sparring between the president on one side and the EPA and the Congress on the other? Partisanship is an important part of the explanation, but not the only part. Another is institutional. All recent presidents have established mechanisms for subjecting major decisions of the EPA and other regulatory bodies to interagency review. Under Nixon and Ford the Office of Management and Budget (OMB)

---

[215] Executive Branch Review of Environmental Regulation, Hearings before the Subcommittee on Environmental Pollution of the Senate Committee on Environment and Public Works, 96 Cong. 1 sess. (Government Printing Office, 1979), pp. 1-2, 231-60, 329-63.

[216] R. Shep Melnick, Regulation and the Courts: The Case of the Clean Air Act, The Brookings Institution, Washington, D.C. (1983), p. 34.

coordinated what it called the "quality of life review," which gave those agencies opposed to EPA actions a chance to attack them. First the Department of Commerce and later the Federal Energy Administration objected to many EPA rules, often delaying their promulgation. President Carter created the Regulatory Analysis Review Group, an interagency committee staffed by personnel from the Council on Wage and Price Stability, to perform similar oversight. President Reagan has reinstituted and strengthened OMB review. While observers disagree on the effect these mechanisms have had on substantive policy, there is little doubt that they have contributed to the hard feelings between the EPA's supporters and those who have established and conducted the review.[217]

Behind these institutional arrangements lies a difference in perspective that often puts presidents at odds with the EPA and its congressional patrons. Presidents are expected not just to protect the environment, but also to promote economic growth, employment, and energy self-sufficiency. They are charged with coordinating the activities of many agencies whose missions bring them into conflict with one another--the EPA, the Department of Energy, the Department of Commerce, the Council of Economic Advisers, and OMB, to name but a few. Thus, presidents, even

---

[217] "Special Report: Office of Management and Budget Plays Critical Part in Environmental Policymaking, Faces Little External Review," 7 *Environment Reporter--Current Developments* 693; Stanley Bach, "Governmental Constraints on Environmental Regulation," in National Academy of Sciences, Decisionmaking in the Environmental Protection Agency, vol. 2b (NAS, 1977), p. 163; and Christopher C. DeMuth, "Constraining Regulatory Costs," *Regulation*, vol. 4 (January-February 1980), p. 13 and (March-April 1980), p. 29.

those who start with strong positions on environmental protection, come more and more to seek what they call "balance," and what their opponents decry as "leniency."[218]

Interest Groups, the States, and Public Opinion

For many years industry kept effective pollution control off the agenda of the federal government. The National Coal Association and the leading automakers spearheaded this opposition. No major environmental group emerged to push for stronger regulation. All this changed in 1970. Industry groups suffered a major setback; they were effectively excluded from decisionmaking on the 1970 Act. New environmental organizations appeared to monitor EPA activities. While industry has slowly recuperated from its defeat, environmental groups have remained remarkably active and strong.[219]

It is difficult to generalize about the role business firms have played in the development of air pollution regulation. The Clean Air Act affects many industries and in different ways. Those especially hard hit by regulation--the auto, steel, nonferrous smelting, and electric power industries--have managed to win delays both from the EPA and from Congress. (The key to Detroit's success was gaining the support of the United Auto

---

[218] R. Shep Melnick, Regulation and the Courts: The Case of the Clean Air Act, The Brookings Institution, Washington, D.C. (1983), p. 35.

[219] R. Shep Melnick, Regulation and the Courts: The Case of the Clean Air Act, The Brookings Institution, Washington, D.C. (1983), p. 35.

Workers.)[220] At first most firms sought above all to avoid making pollution control expenditures at their own facilities. More recently, as this has become harder to achieve, trade associations and broader industry coalitions have grown in number and influence. They have met with mixed success. The newly formed American Industrial Health Council successfully opposed the carcinogen policy proposed by the EPA in 1979. The American Petroleum Institute waged a campaign for a major relaxation of the national standard for ozone (smog), but succeeded only in making the standard slightly more lenient. The Lead Industries Association lost its battle against a stringent standard for airborne lead; the Utilities Air Regulatory Group failed to defeat a restrictive standard for coal-burning power plants in 1979. The Business Roundtable and a new coalition called the National Economic Development Association have focused on convincing Congress to prune the Act. They have yet to achieve a significant legislative victory.[221]

Industry has had greatest success resisting pollution controls when it has enlisted the aid of state governments. The Clean Air Act states that the states, not the federal government, bear "primary responsibility" for controlling pollution. It gives them authority to write and enforce state implementation plans. Since

---

[220] Norman J. Ornstein and Shirley Elder, Interest Groups, Lobbying and Policymaking (Congressional Quarterly Press, 1978), chap. 6.

[221] For a discussion of why industry lobbying is sometimes less effective than one might expect, see Raymond A. Bauer, Ithiel de Sola Pool, and Lewis Anthony Dexter, American Business and Public Policy: The Politics of Foreign Trade, 2d ed. (Aldine, 1972).

state agencies provide much of the personnel, money, and expertise in this exercise in "cooperative federalism," federal regulators cannot ignore their opinions. State governors and legislators frequently offer instructions to these state agencies.[222]

Although several states have developed highly competent regulatory agencies and stringent pollution controls, most are sensitive to the threat of losing jobs as a result of industry closing or relocating. Nevada and Arizona have refused to impose strict requirements on nonferrous smelters, which face serious foreign competition and constitute the largest--or the only--employer in some western towns. Ohio, an economically depressed state highly dependent on electric power generated from the burning of coal, has for years opposed the EPA's efforts to reduce sulfur dioxide emissions. Strangely enough, the states' desire to protect employment does not always put them at odds with environmentalists. For example, many eastern states struggling to retain existing industry have supported programs that impose greater restrictions on pollution in the West and the Sun Belt.[223]

In contrast to industry and the states, environmental groups are relatively few in number and united in purpose. They have worked hard to establish close links with EPA officials, congressional committee members and staff, and the national

---

[222] R. Shep Melnick, Regulation and the Courts: The Case of the Clean Air Act, The Brookings Institution, Washington, D.C. (1983), p. 36.

[223] Ibid.

media. They have also made extensive use of the federal courts.[224]

Environmental groups active in air pollution control include both old-line conservation organizations and younger public interest groups. The most important of the former is the Sierra Club, which led the fight to limit pollution in the Rocky Mountains. Others include the National Audubon Society and the National Wildlife Federation. The environmental groups that have most closely monitored regulation under the Clean Air Act are the Natural Resources Defense Council (NRDC) and the Environmental Defense Fund (EDF), two organizations formed in the late 1960s largely through grants from the Ford Foundation. Both have combined litigation with lobbying Congress and the EPA. While the EDF has emphasized regulation of hazardous pollutants, especially carcinogens, the NRDC has specialized in matters relating to national air quality standards and state implementation plans. A variety of other groups, including the American Lung Association, the League of Women Voters, and a few labor unions, have united with these core groups to form the National Clean Air Coalition, which tries to present a united front to Congress and the media. Their ability to agree on a common course of action has been a key to their success.[225]

Environmentalists have had to deal with two problems in

---

[224] R. Shep Melnick, Regulation and the Courts: The Case of the Clean Air Act, The Brookings Institution, Washington, D.C. (1983), p. 37.

[225] R. Shep Melnick, Regulation and the Courts: The Case of the Clean Air Act, The Brookings Institution, Washington, D.C. (1983), p. 37.

achieving this unanimity. The first is the different priorities of various groups. While some groups (the "smoggies") emphasize the goal of reducing urban pollution, others (the "greenies") seek above all to protect wilderness areas. Policies aimed at reducing urban pollution by encouraging industrial relocation threaten to divide these two groups. Second, maintaining organizations based on what James Q. Wilson has called "purposive incentives" requires emphasizing the threat of immediate and serious danger to the environment.[226] Rhetoric used and positions taken to build support for the organization can make negotiation with agency officials, industry spokesmen, and congressmen difficult. Environmental groups have coped with these problems by stating ambitious environmental protection goals--aimed not just at reducing air pollution but at reducing automobile use and encouraging land-use planning--while accepting long delays in their achievement. They have managed both to paint environmental issues in symbolic terms (pitting the moral goods of health and respect for nature against the evils of pollution and the quest for corporate profits) and reach pragmatic agreements with those whose support they need.[227]

Another reason environmental groups have remained

---

[226] James Q. Wilson, Political Organizations (Basic Books, 1973), chaps. 3 and 9. Also see Jeffrey Berry, Lobbying for the People: The Political Behavior of Public Interest Groups (Princeton University Press, 1977); and David Vogel, "The Politics of the Public Interest Movement," Hudson Institute Paper HI-2950-P (December 1978).

[227] R. Shep Melnick, Regulation and the Courts: The Case of the Clean Air Act, The Brookings Institution, Washington, D.C. (1983), pp. 37-38.

politically influential is that public opinion has continued to support aggressive pollution control. A 1979 poll found that 54 percent of its sample agreed with the statement that "protecting the environment is so *important* that requirements and standards cannot be too high, and continued improvements must be made *regardless* of cost." Of the respondents, 53 percent thought the government was moving too slowly to clean up the air, and only 5 percent thought it was moving too fast. A 1981 Harris poll found that 80 percent of the public oppose any relaxation of the Clean Air Act; 65 percent oppose any cost-based constraint on health standards.[228]

Public opinion on pollution control in part rests on perceptions of who is paying for it. The national media have usually focused on the harm caused by pollution and implied that control costs will be taken out of profits, not passed along to consumers. When the EPA has imposed controls that fall directly on private citizens (such as restrictions on driving or threats to close down a factory), it has met stiff popular opposition. The agency has learned to avoid such measures. In recent years industry has tried to change public perceptions on environmental issues, charging that the real battle lines are between the vast majority of consumers and workers on the one hand and a small minority of environmental purists and individuals with arcane respiratory ailments on the other. How an issue is framed--as an environmental issue, a consumer issue, an employment issue, an energy issue, or a local control issue--often determines who wins and who loses. So far, environmental groups have been far more

---

[228] *Public Opinion*, vol. 2 (August-September 1979), pp. 22-23; *Environment Reporter--Current Developments* 789.

effective in framing issues than have their opponents.[229]

THE EPA: THE ADMINISTRATIVE CORE

Despite the specificity of the Clean Air Act and the extensive oversight performed by Congress and the executive branch, it is the EPA that must apply the words of the statute and find solutions to environmental and administrative problems not recognized by legislators. The EPA is the largest federal regulatory agency, as well as one of the newest and most controversial. In 1970 President Nixon created the EPA by pulling together administrative units from the Departments of Agriculture, Interior, and Health, Education and Welfare. By 1980 it employed over 10,000 people and spent more than $3 billion annually. While air pollution control is the EPA's single largest program, the agency is also responsible for regulating water pollution, noise, pesticides, solid waste, toxic substances, radiation, and hazardous waste.[230]

Within the EPA air pollution policy is made jointly by a number of administrative components. The most visible decisionmakers are the agency's political executives: the administrator, the deputy administrator, and the several assistant administrators responsible for specific program areas. All are appointed by the president and are formally accountable to him.

---

[229] R. Shep Melnick, Regulation and the Courts: The Case of the Clean Air Act, The Brookings Institution, Washington, D.C. (1983), p. 38.

[230] Alfred Marcus, Promise and Performance: Choosing and Implementing an Environmental Policy (Greenwood Press, 1980), pp. 31-49.

The four EPA administrators--William Ruckelshaus (1971-73 and again in 1983), Russell Train (1974-77), Douglas Costle (1977-81), and Anne Gorsuch Burford (1981-83)--have all been lawyers, though with varying degrees of familiarity with pollution control. William Ruckelshaus's lack of experience in the area originally made environmentalists skeptical. By taking aggressive positions on a number of issues in his first year, however, he both established the EPA's reputation as a defender of the environment and developed pride and a sense of mission within the EPA. Russell Train, previously chairman of the Council on Environmental Quality and subsequently president of the Conservation Foundation, expanded the EPA's regulatory programs and kept the agency at arm's length from the White House. Douglas Costle, who had headed Connecticut's Department of Environmental Protection, became known as a manager and mediator. The appointment of Anne Gorsuch Burford reversed the trend toward increasing experience in environmental protection and interrupted the pattern of administrators opposing major relaxation of environmental regulation.[231]

The units that offer advice to the administrator on air pollution questions have frequently been shifted around on organizational charts (receiving a new name each time), but their number and characteristics have remained relatively stable. An assistant administrator heads the agency's air program office. Most have been lawyers and strong environmental advocates. During the Carter administration, for example, David Hawkins, a chief litigator for the NRDC, served in this position. The most

---

[231] R. Shep Melnick, Regulation and the Courts: The Case of the Clean Air Act, The Brookings Institution, Washington, D.C. (1983), p. 39.

important bureau under this assistant administrator's control is the Office of Air Quality Planning and Standards (OAQPS), located in Durham, North Carolina.[232]

More than distance separates the OAQPS from Washington. It is an organization composed of technical personnel: mechanical and chemical engineers, meteorologists, and other specialists. While the EPA's Washington office tends to view the OAQPS as too cautious, the OAQPS tends to distrust the adversarial techniques of lawyers and to suspect that Washington fails to understand technical issues. The tenure of most agency lawyers and political executives is between two and four years, but OAQPS personnel stay much longer. Many current OAQPS officials came to the EPA from the National Air Pollution Control Administration. The OAQPS expects results in years, not months. Moreover, it generally seeks engineering solutions and hesitates to attempt to spur innovation by writing technologically infeasible regulations. Seeing themselves as air pollution control professionals, OAQPS officials have resisted efforts to use the Clean Air Act to achieve ends other than pollution reduction--such as reducing reliance on the automobile or stimulating land-use planning. These attributes have caused friction between the OAQPS and the assistant administrator and have led to the creation of special-purpose units directly under the control of the assistant administrator.[233]

Separated from the air office are those lawyers and

---

232 Ibid., pp. 39-40.

233 In 1974, for example, Assistant Administrator Roger Strelow created the Office of Transportation and Land Use Planning, removing these responsibilities from the OAQPS.

engineers whose job it is to enforce EPA regulations. The Office of Enforcement has a small staff in Washington and many more people scattered throughout the ten regional offices. The Office of Enforcement has an institutional preference for tough, even infeasible, regulations: such rules can improve the agency's bargaining position in negotiations with polluters. Enforcers deal with the hard cases--the "bad apples"--and consequently tend to view polluters as the enemy and negotiations over SIP requirements as the battlefield. The Office of Enforcement has generally opposed attempts to revise SIP provisions, both because such revisions create temporary uncertainty and because this office has a larger role in informal revisions of SIPs (through the negotiating of consent decrees) than in the formal revision process, which is dominated by dispersion modelers in the OAQPS. Envorcement lawyers who expect quick environmental victories usually leave the agency after a year or two of fighting what seem to be never-ending battles against sophisticated polluters. Those who remain--especially in the regional offices--gradually develop the long-range perspective and more accommodating views of the OAQPS's professionals.[234]

While lawyers in the Office of Enforcement prepare the agency's suits against polluters, the Office of General Counsel (OGC) defends the agency from legal challenges.[235] The OGC

---

[234] R. Shep Melnick, Regulation and the Courts: The Case of the Clean Air Act, The Brookings Institution, Washington, D.C. (1983), pp. 40-41.

[235] The Office of General Counsel has from time to time been put under the same assistant administrator as the Office of Enforcement. These reorganizations, though, have not altered the tasks or perceptions of the two offices.

carries more prestige than the Office of Enforcement. Its lawyers are young, ambitious, and eager to set environmental policy. The OGC forms the bridge between the courts and the rest of the agency. It explains the agency's position to reviewing courts and explains to the agency what the courts require it to do. Because the courts have played such an active role under the Clean Air Act, the OGC has a hand in almost every major decision the agency makes. At times OGC lawyers have been more interested in pleasing reviewing courts than in devising workable control programs. This is not surprising in light of their lack of technical background and the fact that they will be blamed if the EPA loses a suit or is found in contempt of court. In the early 1970s OGC lawyers developed a reputation as aggressive "Young Turks."[236]

In recent years a new force has arisen to challenge the preeminence of lawyers within the EPA: the economists. The Office of Planning and Management, staffed by economists and systems analysts, was originally established by Administrator Ruckelshaus to respond to the criticism EPA regulation received in interagency review. As the economic and energy consequences of EPA rules have grown and as opposition to environmental regulation has stiffened, the Office of Planning and Management has gained institutional stature. This office carries on a running dialogue with the Department of Energy, OMB, the president's Council of Economic Advisers, industry lobbyists, and the EPA's academic critics. The Office of Planning and Management has pushed the EPA to develop quantitative analysis for evaluating the benefits and costs of regulation. In recent years the administrator has relied more heavily on the assistant administrator for planning

---

[236] R. Shep Melnick, Regulation and the Courts: The Case of the Clean Air Act, The Brookings Institution, Washington, D.C. (1983), p. 41.

and management for advice that is in tune with the political mood of the country.[237]

Much of the important work of administering the Clean Air Act takes place in the EPA's regional offices. Regulation is decentralized both because pollution problems vary greatly from area to area and because substantial responsibility under the Act rests with the states. The regional offices constitute a bridge between the states and the EPA's Washington office. Regional officials must become familiar with state programs and politics, explain the EPA's regulations to the states, and express state and local concerns to those who set agency policy. Not surprisingly, regional officials are often torn between their dedication to consistent rule application on the one hand and their desire to recognize distinctive local problems and to cut through red tape on the other. Many of the tensions within the Clean Air Act are felt most keenly at this organizational level.[238]

With all these offices involved in making decisions on air pollution control, coordination becomes a problem. The EPA has developed interoffice working groups and a steering committee of senior officials to facilitate discussion and review. One consequence of these various levels of review, though, is delay. Controversial regulations often sit on the back burner for months while participants either look for compromises or try to avoid

---

[237] R. Shep Melnick, Regulation and the Courts: The Case of the Clean Air Act, The Brookings Institution, Washington, D.C. (1983), p. 41.

[238] R. Shep Melnick, Regulation and the Courts: The Case of the Clean Air Act, The Brookings Institution, Washington, D.C. (1983), p. 42.

difficult issues altogether. At times it takes a dramatic event--such as a court order--to force the agency to make a decision.[239]

As important as it is to understand the different perspectives EPA officials bring to policymaking, one should not forget that the EPA is a single organization with a distinctive sense of purpose. Throughout the 1970s almost all agency personnel shared a strong commitment to environmental protection. While recognizing the shortcomings of the Clean Air Act, the agency defended its air program vociferously. Few within the EPA recommended sweeping changes. To some observers this represents bureaucratic inertia and entrenchment: no one wants to change an elaborate program he has spent years building up. But it also reflects a recognition that industry and the states have made major investments with the expectation that existing regulations will remain in place. Rapid change can be unfair, economically wasteful, and administratively disastrous.[240]

Contributing to the EPA's defense of the Clean Air Act was a surprisingly strong and pervasive siege mentality. Despite the support the EPA received from Congress and the steady expansion of its programs, EPA officials saw enemies everywhere. Former Assistant Administrator Robert Sansom expressed vividly the prevalent attitude:

> Most in Congress lacked the vision to see the problem, much less the solution. The few who did understand

---

[239] Ibid.

[240] R. Shep Melnick, Regulation and the Courts: The Case of the Clean Air Act, The Brookings Institution, Washington, D.C. (1983), p. 42.

> EPA's plight were fearful of opening any environmental legislation for amendment. They were afraid because the anti-environmental energy forces in the Congress might have been able to turn an effort to devise national growth, land-use, and transportation policies consistent with a clean environment into an effort to overturn the finest set of laws in the world for abating industrial pollution.[241]

The overriding desire to save the Clean Air Act led the EPA not to disregard political opposition, but, when possible, to avoid it. This occasionally put the agency at odds with pro-environmental congressmen and their staffs. While agency officials may have agreed with the objectives of this group, they realized that the EPA and the Clean Air Act, not individual congressmen or staff members, would receive the blame for overly stringent requirements or mistakes. For this reason, the EPA resisted being pushed too hard by environmental enthusiasts and avoided going to the mat with politically powerful opponents.[242]

The Regulatory Scheme

The Act that the EPA fought so hard to preserve provided the framework within which most policy disputes were resolved during the 1970s. It also created innumerable headaches for agency officials. The authors of the 1970 Act made two key choices that have guided the nation's pollution policy ever since.

---

[241] Sansom, New American Dream Machine, p. 20.

[242] R. Shep Melnick, Regulation and the Courts: The Case of the Clean Air Act, The Brookings Institution, Washington, D.C. (1983), p. 43.

First, they chose to impose direct controls on polluters. Rather than offer subsidies for pollution control, impose taxes on pollution, or establish a system of marketable emission rights, Congress and the executive branch opted--almost without thought--for what has become known as "command and control" regulation. Second, the Act established an ambient air quality, or air quality management, approach to regulation. Congress did debate the merits of this scheme and its alternative, one that sets performance standards based on "available technology." The 1970 Act applied the latter approach to new sources but not to existing sources. To understand the ensuing conflicts over implementation of the Act it is essential to understand the implications of the ambient air quality scheme.[243]

While an emission-based approach to regulating air pollution starts with a definition of "available technology," an ambient approach starts with standards for local air quality (for example, a maximum hourly average concentration of 0.12 part per million of ozone) and sets emission limitations for each pollution source on that basis. Focusing directly on air quality has several advantages. It ensures that polluters who locate in relatively unpopulated and clean areas will not be burdened with the expensive control requirements appropriate for heavily industrialized areas where pollution levels threaten the health of millions of citizens. Conversely, it prevents new polluters from further degrading air quality in those areas where the air is already unhealthy. Politically, stressing air quality makes it easier to present pollution control as a health measure--and few issues are more attractive than protection of the public health. At the same

---

[243] R. Shep Melnick, Regulation and the Courts: The Case of the Clean Air Act, The Brookings Institution, Washington, D.C. (1983), p. 43.

time, setting national air quality standards rather than national emission standards gives the states the opportunity to choose any pollution control mix adequate to meet these standards.[244]

Despite these advantages, the EPA has slowly moved away from the ambient approach under the Clean Air Act. Congress also rejected the ambient approach when it passed legislation on water pollution control in 1972. The reason for this is that regulation based on ambient standards is technically and administratively complex and is based on several assumptions that do not hold up under careful scrutiny. This becomes apparent when one looks at the three stages of regulation under this approach: setting air quality standards, writing individual emission limitations, and bringing sources into compliance.[245]

Standard Setting: The Threshold Problem

The Clean Air Act requires the EPA to set primary (health-based) and secondary (welfare-based) national ambient air quality standards for all those pollutants emitted by "numerous sources" that "endanger the public health and welfare." By 1980 the EPA had established standards for seven criteria pollutants, so named because the EPA must set them after reviewing criteria documents on their effects. These standards are uniform throughout the entire country; the same standard that applies to Littleton, New Hampshire, also applies to New York City and Los Angeles. The 1970 Act allowed heavily polluted areas to apply for two-year

---

[244] R. Shep Melnick, Regulation and the Courts: The Case of the Clean Air Act, The Brookings Institution, Washington, D.C. (1983), p. 44.

[245] Ibid.

extensions of the 1975 deadline for meeting health-based standards, but by 1977 every air pollution control region was expected to attain the primary standards.[246]

Since existing pollution levels vary greatly from area to area, so too does the cost of meeting the standards. Many areas complied with the Act simply by requiring utilities to burn lower-sulfur coal. But Los Angeles could have attained the ozone and carbon monoxide standards only by reducing auto traffic by about 90 percent--a reduction that would have wreaked havoc with that city's entire economic and social structure. Generally the marginal cost of pollution control--the cost of removing the final pound of a pollutant--rises rapidly as the extent of control increases.[247]

The authors of the 1970 Act justified imposing very heavy costs on some areas by claiming that primary standards represent the minimum air quality necessary to protect public health. Primary standards are not based on cost-benefit analysis, but on a medical determination of safe pollution levels. Even if it were possible to find such safe levels, it would not necessarily make sense to spend huge amounts of money achieving these levels instead of using these resources for, say, hospitals or dental clinics.[248] Basing pollution control programs on uniform national

---

[246] R. Shep Melnick, Regulation and the Courts: The Case of the Clean Air Act, The Brookings Institution, Washington, D.C. (1983), pp. 44-45.

[247] Ibid., p. 45.

[248] James E. Krier, "The Irrational National Air Quality Standards: Macro- and Micro-Mistakes," 22 UCLA *Law Review* 323 (1974).

standards becomes even more questionable when one realizes that it is usually impossible to set a "safe" pollution level.[249]

Most scientists now agree that for most pollutants there is no health effects threshold, that is, a concentration below which there are no serious health effects and above which there are. In the words of a study conducted by the National Academy of Sciences, "health damage varies with the upward and downward variations in the concentration of the pollutant, with no sharp lower limit."[250] The House Commerce Committee's 1977 report concluded that "the 'safe threshold' concept is, at best, a necessary myth to permit the setting of some standards."[251] The arbitrariness of any nonzero air quality standard makes it difficult for the EPA to justify its demands that polluters spend large amounts of money to attain it. It also calls into question the wisdom of allowing pollution levels to rise to the national standards in areas currently below them. Thus, the national standards, the foundation of the air quality scheme, may be too lenient for some areas and too stringent for others.[252]

---

[249] R. Shep Melnick, Regulation and the Courts: The Case of the Clean Air Act, The Brookings Institution, Washington, D.C. (1983), p. 45.

[250] National Academy of Sciences--National Academy of Engineering, Air Quality and Automobile Emission Control (GPO, 1974), vol. I, p. 17.

[251] Clean Air Act Amendments of 1977, H. Rept. 95-294, 95 Cong. 1 sess. (GPO, 1977), p. 111.

[252] R. Shep Melnick, Regulation and the Courts: The Case of the Clean Air Act, The Brookings Institution, Washington, D.C.

Emission Limitations: Dispersion and Transport Problems

An effective pollution control program requires clear, specific emission limitations for each pollution source. It is nearly impossible to prove that a particular polluter has contributed to a violation of an ambient air quality standard on any given day. Usually the combined emissions of a number of sources cause such violations. The relative size of their contributions depends on a number of variables, including daily operation levels and weather patterns. Moreover, enforcement action taken against those causing ambient air violations always comes too late; the harm has already occurred. Consequently, the Clean Air Act requires state implementation plans to contain specific "emission limitations, schedules, and timetables for compliance with such limitations," which are enforceable even without a showing that a source caused a particular ambient violation.[253]

The Act gives the states the job of writing emission limitations sufficient to attain national standards, but requires the EPA to make sure these plans are adequate. The first problem that the states and the EPA face is that techniques for plotting the dispersion of pollutants through the atmosphere are highly inexact. In 1971 most states used crude "rollback" models to estimate required emission reductions. If the pollution concentration in the most heavily polluted part of the state exceeded the standard by *x* percent, then all polluters in the state (or at least in that control

---

(1983), pp. 45-46.

[253] R. Shep Melnick, Regulation and the Courts: The Case of the Clean Air Act, The Brookings Institution, Washington, D.C. (1983), p. 46.

region) would be required to reduce their emissions by *x* percent. While such calculations are simple, the worst-case assumptions built into rollback analysis frequently led to more control than necessary to meet the standards.[254]

As polluters and state agencies searched for ways to reduce control requirements, they relied more heavily on dispersion models. Dispersion models are computer simulations that predict how the plumes emanating from smokestacks will be dispersed through the atmosphere. Modeling is technically complex, expensive, and inexact. Even the best models supplied with extensive monitoring data may underpredict actual concentrations by 50 percent or overpredict by as much as 100 percent. Models vary widely in their assumptions and predictive ability. For every model the EPA produces that shows a violation of a national standard, industry can usually find one that predicts that no violation will occur. Such modeling battles can go on for years.[255]

Predicting air quality levels is even more difficult for secondary pollutants, that is, pollutants formed by the interaction of two or more precursors. Ozone (smog) is produced in a complex chemical reaction involving several components, including hydrocarbons and nitrogen oxides. The amount of ozone produced by given quantities of these two components depends on temperature, humidity, and the presence of various catalysts. Similarly, sulfur dioxide, particulate matter, and other pollutants

---

[254] R. Shep Melnick, Regulation and the Courts: The Case of the Clean Air Act, The Brookings Institution, Washington, D.C. (1983), p. 46.

[255] Ibid., pp. 46-47.

combine to produce various forms of sulfates. Most health experts consider the complex sulfate molecule far more dangerous to health than sulfur dioxide. Moreover, the acid precipitation caused by the joining of sulfur dioxide derivatives with moisture in the air decreases the pH of lakes and streams, killing fish and plant life.[256]

Secondary pollutants not only make it difficult to predict how much pollution will be created, but also make it nearly impossible to determine with precision where this pollution will settle. Pollutants emitted in New York City may not create ozone until they reach Hartford, Connecticut. Recent evidence has shown that ozone can travel hundreds, even thousands, of miles in the upper atmosphere. Sulfur dioxide and particulate matter, too, travel hundreds of miles in the upper atmosphere, becoming more dangerous the longer they remain in the air. This phenomenon has become known as long distance transport. Increases in the amount of pollution so transported have become known as atmospheric loading.[257]

These difficulties not only strain the technical capacity of state and federal regulations, but call into question the local basis of air pollution control under the Clean Air Act. By regulating local air quality levels the Act assumes that what goes up in one state comes down in that state. It offers no effective recourse to states such as those in New England that receive the acid rain and high sulfate levels produced by coal burning in states such as Ohio

---

[256] R. Shep Melnick, Regulation and the Courts: The Case of the Clean Air Act, The Brookings Institution, Washington, D.C. (1983), p. 47.

[257] Ibid.

and Illinois. The exporting of pollution has added to the demands for uniform emission limitations on all sources regardless of their location.[258]

Enforcement: Administrative Overload

Thousands of stationary sources and millions of mobile sources pour pollutants into the atmosphere. Although meeting the Act's air quality standards requires that a large number of sources install costly pollution controls, many polluters have delayed spending money on these controls until forced to do so by the government. With so many sources initially in violation of SIP requirements, noncompliance has carried little stigma. This meant that in many areas of the country the states and the EPA had to undertake a massive administrative effort, first to inform polluters of their responsibilities and then to threaten sanctions against those who balked. Success in such an undertaking requires that applicable regulations be known, clear, achievable, and testable; that enforcement resources be commensurate with the task; and that sanctions for noncompliance be credible. Unfortunately, this has not been the case.[259]

The Act gave the states little more than a year to write their SIPs. Most state plans included broad requirements that state agencies expected to tailor to particular sources as the occasion

---

[258] R. Shep Melnick, Regulation and the Courts: The Case of the Clean Air Act, The Brookings Institution, Washington, D.C. (1983), p. 47.

[259] R. Shep Melnick, Regulation and the Courts: The Case of the Clean Air Act, The Brookings Institution, Washington, D.C. (1983), pp. 47-48.

arose. Many such occasions arose when the Arab oil embargo caused the price of low-sulfur fuel to skyrocket, when sources such as steel mills realized that they could not possibly meet their SIP limitations no matter how much they spent, when smelters and paper mills claimed they would go out of business unless the states relaxed control requirements, and when state and federal enforcement officials learned that most state plans did not include definitions of test methods that would allow them to prove that a violation had indeed occurred. The states granted (and the EPA often approved) revision after revision, changing not just cleanup schedules but final control requirements as well. At times it became impossible just to locate the applicable regulation--to say nothing of understanding or enforcing it. When the EPA disapproved a revision, the source could challenge its dispersion modeling. Industry had a strong incentive to cause as much uncertainty as possible, since serious enforcement efforts could not begin until the regulations were clearly established.[260]

The EPA did not have a large enough enforcement staff to inspect or insist upon compliance by more than a small percentage of polluters. It had to rely on the states for most enforcement. To make matters worse, it did not have authority to ask for civil penalties until 1977. This meant the EPA depended on both federal district court judges and the states to get tough with polluters. Generally they did not. The EPA itself often backed away from aggressive enforcement, realizing that trying to shut down many factories would invite congressional backlash. Thus all the shortcomings of the statutory pollution control scheme--technical, economic, and political--became evident in enforcement.

---

[260] R. Shep Melnick, Regulation and the Courts: The Case of the Clean Air Act, The Brookings Institution, Washington, D.C. (1983), p. 48.

Serious enforcement did not start until about 1975, the year the standards were to be achieved. Given the problems created by the Act, it is a tribute to the EPA and state agencies that it took place at all.[261]

The Evolution of Regulation

Regulation of air pollution went through three phases in the 1970s, each corresponding roughly to the term of office of the incumbent administrator and president, and each punctuated by the enactment of new legislation. The period of organization and experimentation lasted from 1970 to 1973, while the EPA was under the direction of William Ruckelshaus. A period of consolidation and growth began with the appointment of Russell Train and the passage of the Energy Supply and Environmental Coordination Act in 1974. In early 1977 a new phase began with President Carter's appointment of Douglas Costle and, later, the passage of the 1977 Amendments. During this period the EPA directed its energies to implementing the Amendments. Enforcement actions became more numerous and regulation became more complex. This era came to a close in 1981 as Anne Gorsuch Burford became administrator and Congress considered further amendments to the Act.[262]

1970-73: Organization and Experimentation

The first years of the EPA and the Clean Air Act were ones

---

[261] Ibid., pp. 48-49.

[262] R. Shep Melnick, Regulation and the Courts: The Case of the Clean Air Act, The Brookings Institution, Washington, D.C. (1983), p. 49.

of confusion, experimentation, and high expectations. The EPA rushed to meet the many deadlines of the Act, promulgating six sets of NAAQS in April 1971, publishing its first NSPS in December 1971, and approving most SIPs on schedule in May 1972. To meet this succession of deadlines the agency based its decisions on any information readily available and tried to put off as many problems as possible. The one air quality standard challenged in court was eventually dropped by the EPA for lack of any scientific justification.[263] The courts also found the EPA's documentation supporting several NSPSs deficient.[264] The SIPs approved in 1972 lacked compliance schedules for individual sources. Facing the dual challenge of enforcing its rules and defending them from attacks, the agency chose to avoid new, controversial tasks, such as writing transportation control plans for major cities. It concentrated its energies on inducing major pollution sources to install technological controls necessary to meet the primary standards as quickly as possible.[265]

Meanwhile events outside the EPA's control had dropped three new issues into its lap. First, the federal courts ordered the EPA to devise a program to prevent the significant deterioration of air quality in areas already meeting primary and secondary

---

[263] *Kennecott Copper Corp. v. Environmental Protection Agency*, 462 F.2d 846 (D.C. Cir. 1972).

[264] *Portland Cement Assoc. v. Ruckelshaus*, 486 F.2d 375 (D.C. Cir. 1973) and *Essex Chemical Corp. v. Ruckelshaus*, 486 F.2d 427 (D.C. Cir. 1973).

[265] R. Shep Melnick, Regulation and the Courts: The Case of the Clean Air Act, The Brookings Institution, Washington, D.C. (1983), pp. 49-50.

standards. The prevention of significant deterioration (PSD) program the agency began to develop in 1973 grew rapidly and quickly became politically controversial. Second, the courts also ordered the EPA to limit automobile traffic in those major cities that could not otherwise meet national standards for carbon monoxide and ozone. These transportation control plans proved to be a disaster that severely wounded the EPA's public reputation. Third, even before the oil embargo of October 1973, the EPA realized that the aggregate SIP-induced demand for clean low-sulfur fuel would exceed near-term supplies. Aware that flue gas scrubbers, even if reliable, take years to design and install, the EPA issued a clean fuels policy that encouraged states with sulfur dioxide regulations more stringent than required by the Act to relax their SIPs in order to make low-sulfur fuel available in areas with higher pollution levels. While the states did little to respond at first, they flooded the EPA with requests for emergency variances once the embargo occurred. By the time Congress began to consider emergency energy legislation in late 1973, the golden years of environmentalism were over.[266]

1974-76: Consolidation and Growth

In the middle years the EPA began to enforce its regulations, to establish extensive new programs, and to implement the provisions of the Energy Supply and Environmental Coordination Act. It beefed up its enforcement staff in the regions and pursued a strategy of seeking informal agreements committing polluters to installation of "reasonably available technology." The EPA conceded that not all areas would be able to meet primary

---

[266] R. Shep Melnick, Regulation and the Courts: The Case of the Clean Air Act, The Brookings Institution, Washington, D.C. (1983), p. 50.

standards by 1975 or even 1977. It asked Congress to extend the deadline and announced its "offset" policy, which allowed some new sources to locate in areas not meeting national standards.[267] Congress waited until 1977 to revise the statutory deadlines and accepted most of the EPA's offset policy.[268]

This period also saw the fall of transportation control plans and the rise of PSD. The transportation plans and related programs ran into so much resistance in 1974-75 that the EPA finally abandoned all pretensions of enforcing them. In 1976 it announced a strategy for controlling mobile source pollutants that deemphasized controls on automobile use. In contrast, agency support for the program to limit pollution increases in relatively clean areas blossomed. The EPA published final PSD regulations in late 1974 and began to issue permits to new sources under this increasingly elaborate scheme. The EPA was slowly moving toward a policy of requiring the use of best available control technology everywhere rather than focusing primarily on those areas exceeding the national standards.[269]

1977-81: Increasing Enforcement and Complexity

---

[267] This policy required new facilities to "offset" their emissions by buying emission rights from existing polluters. 41 Fed. Reg. 55558 (1976).

[268] R. Shep Melnick, Regulation and the Courts: The Case of the Clean Air Act, The Brookings Institution, Washington, D.C. (1983), pp. 50-51.

[269] R. Shep Melnick, Regulation and the Courts: The Case of the Clean Air Act, The Brookings Institution, Washington, D.C. (1983), p. 51.

While most EPA officials and congressmen expected mid-course corrections to the Clean Air Act to pass in 1976, a filibuster by senators opposed to PSD delayed congressional action until 1977. In large part that legislation ratified changes made informally by the EPA. It replaced the original 1975 and 1977 deadlines with more realistic ones geared to the seriousness of particular pollution problems. It also gave the agency new enforcement powers, including civil penalties. With these powers, the backing of Congress, and the support of the Carter administration, the EPA made major strides toward putting some of the nation's worst polluters on compliance schedules. By 1980 almost all air pollution control regions had met primary standards for stationary source pollutants (sulfur dioxide and particulate matter), though not for mobile source pollutants (ozone and carbon monoxide).[270]

The 1977 Amendments also added new and administratively burdensome requirements for PSD, visibility protection, plan revisions for nonattainment areas, transportation control measures, nonferrous smelter orders, and mandatory assessment of noncompliance penalties. As a result the EPA's air program has grown enormously in size and complexity. By 1981 state air officials and the EPA itself joined industry in requesting further legislative action to simplify regulation. Such revisions had not appeared by the time the Ninety-Seventh Congress adjourned in December 1982.[271]

---

[270] Ibid.

[271] R. Shep Melnick, Regulation and the Courts: The Case of the Clean Air Act, The Brookings Institution, Washington, D.C. (1983), p. 51.

A decade of federal regulation of air pollution has produced substantial achievements. The number of violations of primary standards has been significantly reduced in urban areas. The President's Council on Environmental Quality reported that between 1974 and 1978 the number of "unhealthy days" in major cities (using a composite index combining levels for five criteria pollutants) decreased by 18 percent, the number of "very unhealthful" days dropped 35 percent, and the number of "hazardous" days declined by 55 percent. Average annual pollution levels and total emissions also dropped, though not as dramatically.[272]

Serious problems remain nonetheless. Many polluters continue to exceed their legal emission limitations. Many areas continue to violate national standards, especially for ozone. Sulfate levels have failed to decline in the Northeast; acid rain might be getting worse. In short, not only has the Act failed to achieve the ambitious goals established in 1970, but new and serious environmental problems have come to light in intervening years.[273]

---

[272] Council on Environmental Quality, Environmental Quality: Eleventh Annual Report of the Council on Environmental Quality (GPO, 1980), p. 147; and Lester B. Lave and Gilbert S. Omenn, Clearing the Air: Reforming the Clean Air Act (Brookings Institution, 1981).

[273] R. Shep Melnick, Regulation and the Courts: The Case of the Clean Air Act, The Brookings Institution, Washington, D.C. (1983), p. 52.

SUGGESTED READING

9 O.A. Caoinalo, The Fifth Amendment privilege against self-incrimination and compulsory self-disclosure under the Clean Air and Clean Water Acts, Boston College Environmental Affairs Law Review, Spr. 1981, at 359-395.

17 Christian G. Cleutinx, European Community Air Pollution Abatement Policy, (Symposium: Acid Rain and Emerging International Norms), University of Toledo Law Review, Fall 1985, at 113-117.

1987 Steven D. Cook, State-Federal Enforcement of the Clean Air Act and Other Federal Pollution Laws: Federal Overfiling on State Enforcement Proceedings, Brigham Young University Law Review, Summer 1987, at 1085-1101.

22 John A. Coppede, The Clean Air Act: Economic and Technological Feasibility in Setting Standards Under Section 112, Land and Water Review, Sptr. 1987, at 397-412.

15 David W. Hoskins, Acid Rain, Emissions Trading and the Clean Air Act Amendments of 1989, Columbia Journal of Environmental Law, Spring 1990, at 329-357.

Richard L. Klimisch, Let's Clean Up Clean Air Legislation, (A Business and Society Special Issue: Corporations and the Environment: Greening or Preening?), Business and Society Review, Fall 1990, at 48-49.

13 Marianne Lavella, The Fight Over the New Clean Air Act Was Just the Start, 53 col. in, National Law Journal, Nov. 12, 1990, at 1, col. 3.

5 Valerie Lee, Interstate sulfate pollution: proposed amendments to the Clean Air Act, Harvard Environmental Law Review, Wntr. 1981, at 71-80.

129 William F. Pedersen, Jr., Why the Clean Air Act works badly, University of Pennsylvania law Review, May 1981, at 1059-1109.

4 Joseph Post, Federal common lawsuits to abate interstate air pollution, Harvard Environmental Law Review, Wntr. 1980, at 117-144.

2 Edwin M. Smith, Introduction: The Statutory Context of the Air Pollution Problem. (Air Pollution Control: Implementing and Amending the Clean Air Act: Second Annual University of Southern California Environmental Law Symposium, February 19, 1983), Journal of Law and the Environment, Sptr. 1985, at 1-4.

59 D.C. Toedt, State checks and balances as essentials of sovereignty in Clean Air Act rulemaking, Texas Law Review, March 1981, at 581-602.

47 David R. Wooley and John Wappett, Cumulative impacts and the Clean Air Act: an acid rain strategy, Albany Law Review, Fall 1982, at 37-61.